GOODBYE, BLUES

GOODBYE, BLUES

Breaking the Tranquilizer
Habit the Natural Way

Bernard Green, Ph.D.

McGraw-Hill Book Company

New York   St. Louis   San Francisco
Hamburg   Mexico   Toronto

This book describes the serious problem of unhealthy dependency on tranquilizers (and similar drugs) and the value of adopting a safe, drug-free plan to deal with stress and anxiety. It is not intended to replace the services of a physician, nor is it meant to encourage diagnosis and treatment of illness, disease, or other medical problems by the layman. Any application of the recommendations set forth in the following pages is at the reader's discretion and sole risk. If you are under a physician's care for any condition, he or she can advise you about whether the program described in this book is suitable for you.

2 3 4 5 6 7 8 9 D O D O 8 7 6 5 4 3 2

LIBRARY OF CONGRESS CATALOGING IN PUBLICATION DATA

Green, Bernard, 1934–
Goodbye blues.
1. Medication abuse—Prevention. 2. Tranquilizing drugs. I. Title.
RM146.G66   616.86'3   80-21551   ISBN 0-07-024337-9

Book design by Andrew Roberts.

To my wife, Judith.
Her love and support have helped make
this book a reality.

Acknowledgments

Thank you to those who helped make this book possible:

Peggy Tsukahira
Dominick Abel
Ted Schwarz
Beverly Russell

Committee on Prescription Drug Misuse
Kathleen Fryer and the Staff of
    the Fryer Research Center

The Huxley Institute
Dr. Donald Douglas, Pills Anonymous
Roy Morser

Contents

GOODBYE,
BLUES

Introduction

You are special.

You've decided to say "Goodbye, blues!"

You've decided to be free of Valium, Librium, and the spectrum of tranquilizing drugs that keep you from being the self you really can be.

You are going to free yourself from depression and anxiety.

This takes courage, and you have it.

Can you do it? Of course you can.

Hundreds of people have come through my office and safely and comfortably given up tranquilizers, sleeping pills, and antidepressants.

Hundreds who have never taken drugs have cast off depression by following my program.

I want to share their successes with you. I want to open alternatives you may not have known were yours to explore.

You are the people in my book.

Their victories are about to be yours.

Every year new tranquilizers and similar drugs enter the market and others are withdrawn in response to declines in sales or adverse publicity. You may find as you read this book that one or more products named are no longer being prescribed. Or your doctor may prescribe a drug that isn't mentioned, and you may wonder whether or not it's safe. These are valid concerns, but the purpose of this book isn't to serve as a compendium about particular drugs.

The basic premise of this book is that tranquilizers, sleeping pills, and antidepressant sedatives simply *aren't necessary to handle the stress of everyday life*. On the contrary, for many people, after periods of prolonged use, *they* become stress factors.

Our biosystems are beautifully designed to assimilate food, sunlight, and water. They keep our bodies functioning and in equilibrium. The food we eat and the vitamin and mineral supplements we take help to ensure physical and emotional stability. Natural light received through the eyes triggers a biochemical calmative in our bodies. That's why walking out-of-doors is salubrious as well as delightful.

If you use the techniques described in this book, including the simple relaxation and meditation exercises and the concept of talking-it-out, you will discover the joy of life free from tranquilizers and other unnecessary pharmaceuticals.

The case histories related in *Goodbye, Blues* are composites based loosely on the stories of scores of clients who have passed through my office during the last twenty years. They are all "true to life," but names and other distinguishing characteristics have been altered to respect the privacy of my patients and their families and associates.

1

Tranquilizer Dependency: A National Epidemic

_− g_

It doesn't matter how you or your loved ones started taking them. Perhaps it was for back pain, or you might not have been sleeping well at night. There may have been tension at work, a death in the family, a divorce or the end of an intense love affair. You were anxious, possibly hurting, and when your doctor gave you the "blues," the "yellows," or one of the other rainbow-hued colors used for tranquilizers, sleeping pills, muscle relaxers, and antidepressants, you felt certain relief was at hand. For each problem there was a different-strength pill. And you found that, for the moment, they really did work. You seemed more relaxed, less troubled, and perhaps found physical relief from pain that had eluded you for weeks or months.

The same thing may have occurred with a friend, a co-worker, or a member of your family. It was innocent, it was doctor-approved, and you noticed an immediate change for the better in your friend or loved one.

Now some time has passed since you traded anxiety for pills. The anxiety has crept back. You take stronger and stronger dosages to accomplish what a single pill may have done at the start. You may feel lethargic, or just the opposite—"hyper." The reaction varies with each person. Your spouse swallows a tranquilizer and seems to nod off into a different world. You may take the very same prescription pill and feel more overwhelmed by the stress of life than you were before you received that first bottle from your pharmacist so long ago. Or the situation might be reversed. Whatever the case, you or someone you know has reached the stage where you are miserable *with* your pills and terrified *without* them.

If it is any comfort, your situation is far from unique. I have treated hundreds of people who came to me because they felt they were overly dependent upon tranquilizers and similar prescription products that have now been shown to be potentially addictive. In every case, the prescribing physician was only at fault in the sense that he or she was acting on the best available medical information. Tragically, the most readily available information your doctor has had to study over the last several years has now been found not always to be in your best interests. This is the result of rapidly changing technology and a better understanding of the pharmaceutical industry, along with other factors I will mention shortly.

Before I show you the problems your doctor has been facing, I want to stress that this book will tell you how to end the nightmare you or someone you know has been enduring. You are an individual, determined to live life without what has now become an unwanted crutch, or you wouldn't be reading this book. There was no way for you to know that when your doctor gave you that first tranquilizer prescription, he was handing you what too frequently becomes a one-way ticket on a train ride into a pit of despair. Now you are going to find the passage out of that pit. The plan presented is safe and effective, and can completely change your life or the life of someone you love—in a few short weeks.

You were given tranquilizers in good faith by your doctor. You took them with the assumption that they were safe, thoroughly tested, and beneficial. However, the passage of time has shown that less was known about their addictive potential than was believed, and that the manufacturers have had a major stake in educating doctors about the options available. In fact, a case could be made for the argument that the quality of health care in America is determined not so much by your doctor's medical education, the support of health care professionals such as nurses and technologists, or the range of available hospital equipment as it is by the role of the pharmaceutical companies.

How long has your doctor been in practice—five years? Ten? Longer? Just as the technology of computers and electronic instruments and other fields has changed radically in that period of time, so has our knowledge of medicine. A doctor in private practice must utilize advertisements in medical journals, information supplied by pharmaceutical detail personnel (a fancy term for salespeople), and seminars to maintain the latest information. Often your doctor will be given samples of new drugs to try, samples he or she assumes are safe and gives to you when appropriate to save you the cost of a prescription. The tremendous time your doctor must spend with you and other patients makes this form of continuing education the most realistic possible.

Most doctors also rely on a book called *Physicians' Desk Reference*, an annually updated guide to all pharmaceuticals, the information in which is supplied by the manufacturers. The book, generally referred to as *PDR*, lists every drug manufactured, its use, potential side effects, and dangers. Doctors rely on *PDR* as a complete and unbiased reference, when in reality it includes only what the pharmaceutical manufacturers choose to list.

Pharmaceutical companies have performed miracles in our lifetime and try to make the majority of their products fit the real needs of the public. Unfortunately, this multibillion-dollar international business is so competitive that at times the companies have created an illness when previously none existed. One such case was reported by Senator Mike Gravel in a 1972 article in *Playboy* magazine: the case of Ritalin, a stimulant manufactured by the CIBA Pharmaceutical Company.

Stimulants such as Ritalin (technically methylphenidate) are meant to improve a person's mood, reduce the effect of fatigue, and otherwise do exactly what a normal night's sleep will do. The results of taking a drug such as Ritalin vary with the patient for whom it is prescribed. Some people go from a mild depression to extreme anxiety when they react adversely to Ritalin. A near-panic condition can be induced if the patient reacts differently from the manner anticipated.

When Ritalin was introduced, even the manufacturer questioned its need, according to a marketing campaign investigated by Senator Gravel in his research on the drug industry and its practices.

To market Ritalin, CIBA launched advertisements in medical journals, introducing doctors to a new illness: Environmental Depression. The advertisements said that daily living is impossible for many to handle. One advertisement that described the causes of Environmental Depression (ED) included the following scenario:

> Air conditioners are turned down, or off. Lights dim. Transportation slows down or stops—usually in a long hot summer. This is when comfort, conveniences, and productivity suffer. So does the emotional outlook of some individuals. Already frustrated by the constant din around them, helpless in the face of situations they can't control, and faced with the daily exposure of bad news and crises, they fall prey to a phenomenon of the times—one that may overwhelm the patient and may cause symptoms of mild depression to occur more frequently.

The advertisement nearly implied that anyone complaining about the weather might be a candidate for Ritalin. People should not learn to cope with everyday stress, it seemed to suggest, because they are suffering from an "illness" for which a pill was designed. The advertisement explained Ritalin's limitations: "Ritalin will not help all depressed patients faced with environmental problems, and it certainly won't change those problems or an individual's response to them. But Ritalin can improve outlook . . . help get your patients moving again."

The thinking of the CIBA chemists and analysis by the National Academy of Sciences–National Research Council as well as other groups led the Food and Drug Administration to change the use of Ritalin. For the first time, Ritalin was considered appropriate for children. The 1979 edition of PDR stated that Ritalin was most effective with children having Minimum Brain Dysfunction, a radically different condition from the original "Environmental Depression." PDR also shows that Ritalin is effective with the sleep disorder narcolepsy and is "possibly effective" for mild depression as well as aspects of senile behavior. Although the drug was ballyhooed for mild depression in 1972, its actual use yielded an only "possibly" rating for mild depression.

Will your doctor or any doctor question the effectiveness of a drug when there is a shift in advertising campaigns and PDR references? Your doctor has long shared with you the trust that if a pharmaceutical product comes on the market it is either completely safe or all side effects are listed in PDR. Doctors do not have the time to handle exhaustive comparative studies even within the pharmaceutical company literature. Unfortunately, if mistakes are made in the literature, or if a side effect such as addiction or dependency is not stressed, it is going to be you, the patient, who suffers.

The Ritalin campaign is an example of the effort pharmaceutical companies make to limit your doctor's awareness of other points of view. Pharmaceutical manufacturers' advertising and promotion budgets allow $5000 per doctor each year to communicate to the medical profession in medical journals. There is an inevitable effect on the trade journals' editorial policies; they couldn't survive without the advertisements, without charging prohibitive prices to their subscribers. It is no surprise that alternatives to drug therapy, such as nutritional controls, are seldom discussed in their pages.

American pharmacists report filling approximately one and a half billion prescriptions annually, which translates to approximately seven prescriptions for every man, woman, and child. Many of these prescriptions are unnecessary. Pharmaceutical advertising suggests to you and your doctor that a pill might be an acceptable panacea. In reality, symptoms such as anxiety, difficulty coping with emotional problems, and sleeplessness can be handled more effectively without medication, as will be explained later in this book.

The plan I have developed to help you, your loved ones, and millions of people just like you does not rely upon pharmaceuticals. It shows you the natural way to use diet, exercise, relaxation techniques, and what I call "talking-it-out" not only to get off all tranquilizers and related, nonessential prescription medication but also to deal with future stress. You have the strength to stand alone, and you have turned to pills only because no one has ever shown how to tap your enormous inner resources. You are in a temporary bind because you did what I have done and millions of others do—listened to the "experts" who are really trying to sell you a product. A simple altering of your lifestyle will not only free your body from the need for tranquilizers, it will also result in your discovering how to use your inner powers to handle future stress without pills.

The New York State Committee on Prescription Drug Misuse has found that at least 90 million prescriptions sold annually in the United States have nothing to do with influenza, pneumonia, cancer, heart disease, or the like. They are given simply to help people calm their nerves. In 1977, 57,084,000 prescriptions were written in the U.S. for just one tranquilizer, Valium. More than three billion Valium pills were dispensed—and that's just one of the many minor tranquilizers prescribed.

The pharmaceutical companies find all kinds of ways to use tranquilizers. For example, doctors and nurses are aware that patients facing hospital surgery will be nervous. They are aware that most patients need only to have the procedures explained to them in order to ease the anxiety. However, leading pharmaceutical manufacturers encourage doctors to use tranquilizers. One advertisement for a widely prescribed tranquilizer suggests its use with "Anxious patients with organic or functional disorders," "Anxious patients facing endoscopic procedures," "Anxious patients scheduled for elective Cardioversion," "Anxious patients facing surgery."

The message is clear. When you are faced with an anxious situation, your doctor should encourage you to take a pill, not help you with sensitive understanding. Giving the pill enables a doctor to spend less time, if any, with the patient before surgery. The nurse simply dispenses medication. The pharmaceutical company makes its money. But the patient experiences the introduction of a foreign substance into the body. This can create separate problems. Adverse reactions are usually not known until *after* the medication has been given.

Valium and other mild tranquilizers have value when limited primarily to the hospital surroundings. However, doctors who prescribe such medication in the hospital frequently let their patients continue taking the pills after they are released, even though long-term use is not safe. The Valium advertisement warns that use for more than four months can have unpredictable results. Even worse, the advertisement admits the possibility of addiction to Valium. One advertisement states: "Withdrawal symptoms (similar to those with barbiturates, alcohol) have occurred following abrupt discontinuance—convulsions, tremor, abdominal/ muscle cramps, vomiting, sweating."

Your doctor did not fail you when you were given your tranquilizer prescription. The warning about possible addiction is downplayed to such a degree that your doctor, like thousands of others, was probably not concerned. Your doctor assumed that the drug would not have been allowed on the market unless it was so safe that addiction was unlikely. To your doctor, the risk was probably not as great as driving a car or operating a power lawnmower.

Another point worth noting is that while tranquilizers are supposed to counter anxiety, some people actually become *more* anxious after taking them.

A typical advertisement for a tranquilizer mentions some problems a doctor might encounter in patients who have

been taking the drug: "hyperexcited states, anxiety, hallucinations, increased muscle spasticity, insomnia, rage, sleep
disturbances, and stimulation have been reported." The
advertisement says that the drug should be discontinued if
these symptoms appear. But doctors often prescribe more of
the drug instead, assuming the patient requires a stronger
dose. If a patient shows anxiety after taking the drug, how is
the doctor to know whether the anxiety is the condition or
the treatment? (These are known as "Paradoxical Reactions.")

Valium is not unique in having side effects that look like
the problem they are treating. PDR's write-up for Librium
states that among the possible adverse reactions are "excite-
ment, stimulation, and acute rage." Other tranquilizers produce similar reactions.

I don't mean this to be an indictment of any particular
drug or drug manufacturer. I am giving you information so
you can better understand how easy and how natural it is to
get into trouble with pharmaceuticals. There is no completely safe tranquilizer in existence at this writing.

Tranquilizers, no matter what the name or manufacturer,
are made up of the same basic chemicals. There are two types
of tranquilizer: minor and major. The minor tranquilizers, of
which Valium is perhaps the best known, are used to
alleviate anxiety and tension, but can cause true physical
and psychological dependency following prolonged use.
The major tranquilizers—Thorazine, Prolixin, and Melloril
are examples—can control the symptoms of psychosis from
partially to a significant degree, but they can also cause
serious neuromuscular side effects.

This problem in its more developed state is called tardive
dyskinesia, which produces abnormal involuntary facial and
body movements such as jerks, tics, and uncontrolled rhyth-
mic movement of the tongue. Sometimes the eyes blink
constantly or the mouth moves so much that normal speech
is difficult. In other cases, the person's feet are constantly
moving in tiny steps, even when seated or standing. The
major tranquilizers are prescribed most frequently for patients diagnosed as psychotic.

Some manufacturers are encouraging broader use of major tranquilizers. A case in point is the Merck, Sharp & Dohme (MSD) advertisement for Triavil, a combination tranquilizer and antidepressant containing the drugs perphenazine and amitriptyline HCl. The advertisement appeared in the May 1979 *Physician's Management* and shows a female business executive playing racquet ball. She is celebrating her birthday with her husband and two children. The headline is "ready to do more, able to do more . . . ," implying that the drug is meant to relieve moderate anxiety without limiting the patient's activities. Other benefits Triavil promises are better concentration and an enhanced sense of well-being on awakening.

This certainly sounds like a wonder drug. On another page in the same magazine, however, the manufacturer listed the possible reactions to the drug it had so enticingly advertised. Among them: "Tardive dyskinesia may appear in some patients on long-term therapy or may occur after drug therapy with phenothiazines and related agents has been discontinued. The risk appears to be greater in elderly patients on high-dose therapy, especially females. *Symptoms are persistent and in some patients appear to be irreversible.* The syndrome is characterized by rhythmical involuntary movements of the tongue, face, mouth or jaw. Involuntary movements of the extremities sometimes occur. *There is no known treatment for tardive dyskinesia;* antiparkinsonism agents usually do not alleviate the symptoms. *It is advised that all antipsychotic agents be discontinued if the above symptoms appear.*" (Italics added.)

In other words, a patient using this drug runs the risk of developing a lifelong affliction after discontinuing it.

It is the chemical family involved, not the manufacturer's degree of skill, that causes this danger. Tragically, individual response to this variety of drugs differs, and the potential problems for any given individual cannot be predicted with certainty.

One reason so many of these tranquilizers have been administered in such large quantities over the years is that patients ask for them. Indeed, patients must share responsibility for the tranquilizer explosion. Many people have developed the attitude that personal problems are best handled externally rather than internally. This attitude is encouraged by the medical profession, which is encouraged by pharmaceutical advertising. Even minor physical or emotional pain, though a normal part of human existence, is somehow "bad" to endure. Rather than live with a cold, a slight headache, or the normal grief process following the loss of a loved one, we should take a pill to feel better.

You must always keep in mind that you have inner strength and internal healing abilities from which you can draw, no matter how little credence you give them now. The reasons you became involved with tranquilizers are complex. You thought you were being rational, based on the best medical information. Unfortunately, that information was wrong. Now you are going to learn a safe, simple, effective way to free yourself from tranquilizers, sleeping pills, and antidepressants. You will learn, in the face of any emotional crisis, how to rely on yourself in the years ahead.

Take the case of Louis, a man who spent ten years on tranquilizers before coming to see me. Louis was twenty-nine years old when he stopped outside his apartment door, bent over to get his morning paper, and felt a sharp pain in his back. When the pain didn't ease, he went to an internist who, after an examination, referred him to a physical therapist in the medical complex where the internist practiced. The therapist said that since the doctor had found no damage to the back, a series of exercises done each day would stop the pain and strengthen the back. The weakness that had caused the injury in the first place was something he would have to deal with for the rest of his life. However, Louis was told to do the exercises first thing in the morning every day. If he did so faithfully, it was unlikely he would ever experience such back pain again. If he stopped the exercise and let his back return to the relatively weakened state it had been in, the pain would be likely to return.

Louis followed the advice for six months and felt marvelous. The exercises took less than five minutes a day, but gradually he drifted away from doing them. Then, a year later, the pain came back. The advice was the same, but this time Louis also talked with a friend. "I don't bother with that exercise nonsense," said the friend. "I take a pill first thing in the morning and I'm fine all day."

Louis decided that a pill was right for him, too, and he talked with his doctor about it. "I can prescribe a tranquilizer like Valium, which is also a muscle relaxer," said the doctor. "But are you sure you want it? The exercise program worked while you were on it. Don't you just want to continue with that and save the cost of the prescription?"

"Why work when a pill will do the same thing?" reasoned Louis, and his doctor gave a prescription.

Ten years later, Louis was so pill-dependent that he experienced severe withdrawal symptoms when he tried to go a day or two without his tranquilizer. Whereas the exercise program had been within his control, the pill now controlled him. Yet he had been the one who insisted on the pill—the instant cure—when there were safe alternatives that did not involve a pharmaceutical.

We have become so accustomed to advertisements for cold capsules, headache tablets, and encapsulated panaceas that when we go to the doctor we expect him or her to prescribe a pill. We don't even think about whether or not relief would come as quickly without the medication as it does with it. We do not consider the alternatives. We don't recognize that *some pills treat only a symptom, not the underlying cause.* We are uncomfortable with doctors who shy away from saying even "Take two aspirin" (an over-the-counter compound that is known to cause internal bleeding, ulcers, and other serious side effects in people with certain sensitivities).

Most of us fail to realize that we have the power to change our health and counter pain, and that we don't need drugs to do it. We do not have to take tranquilizers to relax or deal with stress, or take a sleeping tablet to sleep. There are natural highs without pills. If you are on pills, there are safe ways to ease off.

You have more potential for happiness, a stress- and pain-free life without tranquilizers, sleeping tablets, and other pills than you have ever realized.

Research into mood-altering ailments in the last twenty years reveals a connection between the amount of nutrients the body receives and emotional health. Orthomolecular psychiatrists and doctors use vitamins, minerals, and nutrients for their emotionally troubled patients.

Even research chemists for pharmaceutical companies are exploring alternatives to tranquilizers. For example, Dr. H. Möhler, a researcher with Hoffman LaRoche in their Basle headquarters, has discovered that nicotinic acid (actually Vitamin B$_3$) appears to have the same tranquilizing properties as a chemical tranquilizer as reported in an article published in an international magazine for scientists and researchers, *Nature*. If subsequent research bears out Dr. Möhler's preliminary findings, we will know that a megadose of a vitamin, with no known side effects, can achieve the same result as a tranquilizer. Findings such as Dr. Möhler's suggest that proper nutrition, not medication, can be the path to a stress-free life.

Mental equilibrium can be achieved naturally even in the face of severe anxiety. The power of megavitamin therapy is graphically demonstrated in the potent effects of the B vitamin with the elderly. A deficiency of Vitamin B complex can cause the physical and mental conditions normally attributed to senility in the elderly. Studies indicate the majority of senile patients show erratic behavior because of improper nourishment rather than organic damage. Instead of prescribing tranquilizers for the antisocial behavior of the "senile," as the manufacturers of pharmaceuticals would recommend, orthomolecular psychiatrists start treatment with massive doses of vitamins such as B complex with C and zinc.

Orthomolecular psychiatrists—who rely heavily on nutrition and megavitamins—stress that the human body is not naturally comprised of Valium, Librium, or any other tranquilizer. There is no such thing as a tranquilizer deficiency.

In contrast, Vitamin B complex and other nutritional factors are natural to the human body. A nutritional deficiency can easily exist, and such deficiencies affect the mind.

The few doctors who recognize that the traditional approach to medical treatment is not the only approach are afraid to reveal alternatives because they'll be criticized by their patients. Take the case of Henry, who had suffered with chronic degenerative rheumatoid arthritis for more than twenty years. The condition began in childhood, when several severe food allergies went undiagnosed. The abnormal fluid loss because of chronic diarrhea caused Vitamin C and Vitamin B complex to be lost. B and C are water-soluble vitamins that are not stored in the body and must be replenished daily. Henry's doctor, though recognizing this fact, placed Henry on a medication program with side effects that included high blood pressure and retina damage leading to eventual blindness.

For years Henry took the prescribed medication, having both blood pressure and eyesight checked every three months as a necessary precaution. However, he learned of information linking nutritional deficiencies with rheumatoid arthritis and suggested to his doctor that a combination of change in diet and vitamin supplements, particularly acid, be tried instead. His doctor scoffed at this and Henry sought a new doctor. Through controlled experiments and careful blood monitoring during the next four years, the arthritis, which had barely been arrested by the medication, was actually eliminated by the diet and vitamins.

Today Henry is not using any drugs. He takes only vitamins and follows a diet high in protein, low in carbohydrates, and devoid of sugar to avoid any onset of arthritis. Medical tests indicate that he is actually free of a problem pharmaceuticals couldn't promise to cure. His original doctor now admits, off the record, that he didn't suggest the dietary alternative himself, though he *was aware* of it, because he was afraid of a malpractice suit. "My patients *expect* me to prescribe pills for their problems. If I suggest a less accepted alternative and they fail to get immediate relief, there is a good chance I can be sued."

Despite all that is known about tranquilizers, they continue to be the major prescription drug recommended and taken for everything from depression following a death to stress to "housewife blues." In 1977, a New York State study of prescription drugs dispensed throughout the United States noted that 32 million women and 19 million men took tranquilizers prescribed by their doctors. This statistic is misleading, because it was also found that the prescriptions were shared. In many offices, if someone complains of anxiety, he or she is offered a tranquilizer by friendly co-workers who have prescriptions.

Social class and level of education are related to tranquilizer use. Tranquilizers, sleeping pills, and antidepressants are not the drugs of the poor and the uneducated. Tranquilizer users are likely to come from the middle- and upper-income strata of society and those educated beyond high school level.

Maturity is also a factor in minor tranquilizer use. Most people who take Valium are over thirty-five and take it for nonmedical reasons—in other words, it was prescribed for anxiety or other symptoms to which a specific illness could not be attributed.

Women appear disproportionately in statistics relating to tranquilizer use because they visit doctors more regularly. Annual Pap tests alone bring women into contact with doctors far more frequently than routine check-ups would bring a man. When a woman comes to the doctor, her minor complaints of nervousness at her job or at home may result in a prescription for a tranquilizer.

A mother with young children talks with the doctor, discusses her problems, hoping she will have a sympathetic ear. But the doctor is often too busy to listen. The average office visit is thirteen minutes. Rather than take the trouble to listen to the mother, the doctor is likely to prescribe a tranquilizer.

Complaints about work, relations with her husband, and other minor difficulties are often handled by doctors in the same manner. The doctor does not want to take an extra five or ten minutes to help the woman talk through the problem.

A doctor's income is determined, in part, by the turnover of patients. The doctor who spends twenty minutes with a female patient rather than the thirteen-minute average cuts his or her income potential by 50 percent. Thus it is more profitable to prescribe a tranquilizer than to listen.

Former First Lady Betty Ford discussed the problem of the doctor too willing to prescribe tranquilizers when she admitted to her own problems of prescription-drug and alcohol addiction in *The Times of My Life* (Harper & Row):

> A tranquilizer or a dry martini, each brings the same relief. . . . And when I say drugs, I'm talking about legal medications, prescribed by doctors.
>
> At first, I was bitter toward the medical profession. Fourteen years of being advised to take pills, rather than wait for the pain to hit. I had never been without my drugs. I took pills for pain, I took pills to sleep, I took mild tranquilizers. Today things are changing, doctors are being educated right along with the rest of us, but some of them used to be all too eager to write prescriptions. It was easier to give a woman tranquilizers and get rid of her than to sit and listen to her.

One survey indicates that one out of five American women between eighteen and twenty-eight, and one out of eight adolescent girls has been given stimulants or sleeping pills for non-specific problems. These statistics are for the women who have received prescriptions for *non-specific* problems— in other words, something other than an actual illness.

Many doctors who prescribe tranquilizers for valid reasons do little or no follow-up. One of my cases was Bill, a rising young bank executive. He started working in a bank right after high school, first as a teller, then switching from department to department as he went to college in the evenings for advanced training. Bill began taking tranquilizers during a stressful period. He was married, with a small baby, studying for his master's degree and in charge of the largest branch bank in the city. His parents died in a car crash. He was unable to deal with the trauma, went to see his doctor, and was given a prescription for Valium.

"The doctor never told me how to take the pills," said Bill, who came to see me three years later, desperate to rid himself of tranquilizer addiction.

He said I should use my judgment. He explained that minor tranquilizers were helpful bridges across deep emotional traumas everyone experiences at some time in their lives. He told me the pills were harmless and that I should use them to cope with the stress I was under. He said that I might need just one or two pills and I might want them more regularly. The choice was up to me, since they could only help me.

I worked through my grief fairly quickly but I found the Valium eliminated so much stress, I didn't want to stop. If the baby was crying when I was trying to study, I'd take one of the pills. I took a pill before going to a meeting with the bank's regional manager and another the day I had a particularly important test at the university. When I ran out, I suspected I was overusing the pills and thought the doctor's office would ask me to come in for an appointment before refilling the prescription. No one cared, though. They just called the pharmacy and told the druggist to give me more. I was even asked if I wanted a larger number this time.

That's how it started. Soon I was taking the Valium all the time, never trying to handle stress that was normal in my job. The Valium was always easier to face than reality.

Eventually my job and marriage were affected by my tranquilizer use. I became irritable without the drug. I would fly off the handle when experiencing minor problems. Sometimes I would find my body trembling in the morning and other times I would feel extremely anxious for what seemed to be no logical reason. I realized I had become dependent upon Valium instead of myself. I hated that feeling. Yet I didn't know what to do.

Bill tried a number of ways to cope before coming to see me. He stopped Valium "cold turkey," experiencing such anxiety and physical distress that he called his doctor for a new prescription. Several other doctors he consulted suggested he switch to either a higher Valium dosage or that perhaps one of the other tranquilizers (such as Librium) would have a more powerful effect. It was only when a coworker mentioned the success she had had with the program in this book that he decided to come to see me. In less than six weeks' time he was off tranquilizers forever.

You can be too.

If you are reading this book, the chances are that you or someone you know has a problem with tranquilizers and the doctor has avoided facing that possibility. Yet you recognize that you or your friend chose to lead a life with a pill handling the problem.

Fortunately there are proven alternatives to tranquilizers, and you will learn how your body can produce a natural calming agent through many processes—one in particular, *photobiology*. Another, a controlled diet coupled with vitamin and mineral supplements, can help you withdraw from tranquilizers slowly, safely, and comfortably. Nutrition is your key to handling unusual stress after you have stopped taking tranquilizers. There are simple physical and meditative exercises you can work into even the busiest schedule.

In the chapters that follow, you will learn how to wean yourself from tranquilizer dependency and feel you don't need them any more, even under high anxiety conditions. This will lead you to a better understanding of your body and its real needs. Proven, effective, harmless alternatives exist. You can be free of tranquilizers forever. I am going to tell you how.

2

Is It Safe
for Me to Stop
Taking Tranquilizers?

There is a myth about tranquilizers, sleeping pills, and antidepressants. Because they are available only through prescription, we tend to think of them as essential weapons in the medical arsenal against disease. We assume they are in the same category as antibiotics, penicillin, and other drugs that cure serious sickness. In reality, some physicians dispense tranquilizers so casually you might think they are as essential to the body as vitamins and minerals. Such doctors refill a patient's prescription for tranquilizers month after month and year after year, inadvertently implying that the patient has a basic "tranquilizer deficiency."

If tranquilizers have become part of your daily routine, they cannot be stopped "cold turkey." If you have been taking any tranquilizer for more than twelve consecutive days, stopping abruptly will cause withdrawal symptoms. If your tranquilizer use has extended over months or years, suddenly flushing the drug down the toilet and trying to live without the pills can cause extreme anxiety, depression, nausea, hyperactivity, and suicidal thoughts. People who function for years in high-pressure, high-paying jobs while

taking tranquilizers find themselves unable to make decisions. In extreme cases, they can find themselves in the
hospital.

Take the case of Janine Haroldson, a pseudonym for a well-
known graphic artist. She became addicted to tranquilizers
and lived in a nightmare world trying to get off them alone
before coming to me for help.

> I never really thought about tranquilizers one
> way or another before. It's not like I hadn't been
> around them. Years ago, when the children were small
> and I had just gone back to work in advertising, my
> husband and I hired Rose, an absolute jewel, who
> cleaned our Manhattan apartment, looked after the
> children when they returned from school and got
> dinner started for Larry and me. She was going
> through a divorce and there were days when her
> problems and the noise of my constantly running
> children got too much for her. She took one or two
> pills and seemed to completely relax. Neither the
> yelling of the children nor her troubles at home
> seemed to matter. She did her work calmly and I got to
> admire the way she was able to cope.
> Many of my friends were taking tranquilizers, too.
> Some had high-pressure jobs with magazines and
> book publishing companies. Others were stay-at-
> home types whose doctors suggested Valium or
> Librium or Miltown when they complained of feeling
> nervous and vaguely uneasy from day to day. The
> pills were always around me, I never thought any-
> thing about my first prescription. It was only later,
> months later, that I had experienced the agony of
> withdrawal, the shakes, the disorientation, the crying
> jags for no reason, that I understood why they call that
> innocent-looking bottle of pills the "blue death."

Janine had experienced a number of extreme setbacks over
the years, all of which she weathered without tranquilizers.
One of her children was born with a heart condition that
required five corrective surgeries. Her husband experienced
business difficulties that tied up his money in international

enterprises to the point that his take-home was actually less than that of his secretary. The pressures were extreme, but they always were manageable without pills.

Gradually life improved for Janine. Her husband became successful and she acquired a high-paying job in advertising. However, her husband also drifted into an affair with a woman in England, where one of his businesses was based, and the couple were divorced.

> Then my daughter dropped out of college where she had made the Dean's list in her first semester [Janine continued]. She moved in with a young musician who had no talent, seldom worked even the smallest clubs in the Boston area where they were living, but whom she said she loved. They planned to travel cross-country, working wherever someone would hire them. It was very romantic to my daughter. I was so upset that I began drinking martinis at lunch, something I had previously done only on rare occasions. When I caught myself drinking during the morning coffee break as well, I went to see Jack, my doctor and friend, who got me off alcohol and onto Valium. He said it would help me control the stress so I wouldn't do something self-destructive, like continuing on the road to becoming an alcoholic. He never realized he was starting me on a path that was just as bad.

Janine's drug use grew gradually. "At first I used only an occasional Valium, saving them for truly high-stress situations. When I finished talking with Larry's lawyer about the divorce settlement, I would reach for the bottle and take one of my blue pills. It didn't stop the pain of the divorce. It didn't prevent the lonely ache of going to bed each night, thinking that somehow I had apparently failed to keep my husband happy. It didn't bring my daughter back to her senses. But it did make the world an easier place in which to live. The stresses never eased. I was just able to ignore them. I wasn't coping any better than I had been. I was just avoiding facing my problems for so long as the drug was in my system."

Eventually Janine realized that she might have a problem. She tried to avoid facing that possibility—as you might have done before you picked up this book, if you are typical of tranquilizer takers—but subconsciously she knew what was happening. As she related:

"Occasionally I wondered about the sense of what I was doing. I talked with Jack, who by then had given me a prescription which could be refilled as often as I wished. 'You're a sensible woman, Janine,' he told me. 'I've known you for what . . . fifteen years now? Twenty years? You're not going to abuse the tranquilizers. You've been going through a stressful period this last year or two. The Valium makes it easier to cope.'

"My friend, my doctor, had become my pusher. . . ."

Janine explained:

The more tranquilizers I took, the more anxious I seemed to become. I was rapidly growing addicted to them, a fact neither Jack nor I recognized. Even worse, I was falling into the trap of cross-addiction. During tours to set up exhibits across the country, I was having trouble with the idea of sleeping in a strange bed in a new hotel room every night. Jack made certain I had sleeping tablets to take so that I would be rested in the morning. I took one pill to get me through the days and another to get me through the nights. On those rare occasions when I ran low on one or the other of my medications while I was out of town, I'd start to panic. Fortunately neither drug was considered harmful by the medical profession and hotel doctors were happy to supply me with prescriptions which could be filled in nearby pharmacies.

My cross-addiction was getting worse as the months passed. I somehow managed to mount my second one-woman exhibit and again it was a success. This time there was talk of creating a set for a feature movie and I flew to Hollywood, fortified by yet more of my "blue death." I began looking for any excuse to take one of the Valium. If the plane was late taking off from the airport, I took a pill to reduce my anxiety about missing my appointment. I took another pill after landing, before going for my luggage, because I was anxious about the chance that one of my bags would be lost and I'd be without a change of clothing. I'd have to go to the producer's office looking like the wrath of God and then what would be my chances of getting the contract? This is not to say I ever lost any luggage, because I didn't. I was just nervous about the possibility and the pills which traveled everywhere with me in my purse were meant for handling that nervousness.

Then one day I did the inevitable. I took too many pills too close together and lost consciousness. I wasn't suicidal or acting deliberately. I just couldn't think clearly any more. I was alone in the apartment, having just put some food on the stove, and passed out on the floor. When I awakened, I went to the couch to lie down. Something important had to be done but I couldn't think clearly enough to know what it was. I didn't remember until the firemen arrived with my son. In my drug-induced stupor, I had let the food on the stove burn to a crisp. The room had filled with smoke and I was later told I was minutes from a serious fire when my son came home from basketball practice and discovered what was happening.

That's it, I told myself. I've become addicted to the tranquilizers. I'm a successful artist in a very competitive field, and even in demand as a public speaker. I don't need Valium or any other crutch. I marched to the bathroom and flushed both the blue death and the sleeping pills down the toilet, my son watching with pride. I had licked blue death! I had conquered my fears! I had . . .

I lasted for two days, the worst forty-eight hours of my life. I didn't sleep. I paced the floor, sweated, and felt as though I was going to convulse. I vomited my food and felt like I was living a nightmare. Thank God my pusher, Jack, was available. I told him I had lost my Valium and he telephoned a prescription to the pharmacy in the building next to where I work. The pharmacist was also aware of the "safety" of minor tranquilizers like Valium, so he didn't seem troubled when I took the first one even before I paid the bill.

Janine's story has a happy ending. She eventually did get off both tranquilizers and sleeping pills. A close acquaintance who had shared her problem made an appointment for Janine to see me. She tried the approach I am about to describe and found that it was the answer she had been seeking. The judicious use of vitamins, a slight diet modification, exercise, and relaxation techniques, all explained later in this book, accomplished for Janine what other approaches had failed to do.

The program outlined in the next two chapters is meant to eliminate the pain and danger of withdrawal. You must not stop taking the tranquilizer instantly, but ease off the drug a bit at a time. You will stop taking pills over a period of weeks so that your body can adjust gradually. This gradual withdrawal eliminates the problems which might otherwise occur and enables you to never know a day of anxiety despite the fact that you have thrown away your chemical "crutch." More important, the chapters ahead show you how to live without tranquilizers, sleeping pills, or antidepressants.

If you follow the plan in this book you will be living tranquilizer-free. You will have conquered the chemical dependency that results from consuming too many tranquilizers over too long a period of time. If you have used tranquilizers and/or sleeping pills as an occasional crutch, you will understand how to live more fully and more freely without that occasional crutch.

You can be free of tranquilizers. You can find the untapped inner resources that eliminate the symptoms for which the drugs were prescribed.

3

The Plan

There are several parts to the plan for getting off tranquil
izers. These include the use of vitamins and minerals, with
an emphasis on choline, one of the B vitamins, to wean
yourself of tranquilizers; exercise; relaxation techniques; a
completely natural process known as photobiology; an approach to interpersonal relations I call "talking-it-out"; and a
change in your nutrition. Once you have liberated yourself
from tranquilizers, you will use particular aspects of this
same program to keep yourself from ever feeling the need for
tranquilizers again.

Whether you are dependent on tranquilizers or have a
cross-dependency or cross-addiction—and remember, alcohol is also considered a drug—the first step is to start cutting
back on your tranquilizer intake. No matter what your
normal dose has been, you should reduce it by a *maximum
of 5 mg per week.* For example, if you take 30 mg of any
tranquilizer daily, during the first week of withdrawal your
daily dose will be at least 25 mg. You can take more if you
need to do so, as long as you are taking less than the 30 mg.
During the second week you may cut back another 5 mg so

that you are down to 20 mg per day. In the third week you take another 5 mg less, and so on throughout the withdrawal period.

Limiting yourself to a maximum reduction in your tranquilizer dosage of 5 mg is the only part of my program that is inflexible. Reducing by more than 5 mg per week raises the risk of serious side effects. Some people find that even a 5-mg reduction leaves them jittery and unable to function as effectively as they would like. If you experience those feelings, try reducing your intake by 3 or 4 mg. You will withdraw more slowly, but more comfortably. What matters is what you feel mentally and physically during your withdrawal, no matter how long it takes.

The vitamin aspect of the program counters the chemical stress resulting from long-term tranquilizer use. Your body will continue to crave its pharmaceutical "fix." The use of choline, part of the B complex vitamins, eliminates the intense craving for a tranquilizer some of my patients experience during withdrawal.

The key vitamin in the fight against tranquilizer addiction is Vitamin B_3, obtainable in a number of forms. One form is niacin, but I never recommend niacin for adults, because taken in quantity it causes a flush and a hot tingling sensation. These reactions are not at all harmful, but may be embarrassing or temporarily discomforting. I recommend obtaining B_3 in the form of niacinamide, which is converted into niacin in the body. Vitamin B_3 is natural to the body. It is nonaddictive and causes no chemical stress. If you take more than your body needs, because it is a water-soluble vitamin, it is expelled daily in your natural waste.

The exercise portion of the program, explained later, is designed to exploit the body's natural tranquilizer—exposure of the eyes to natural light, which is converted by the body to Vitamin D, a natural calmative.

The talking-it-out section of the program will teach you how to put your problems into perspective. In more than twenty years of practice as a psychotherapist, having seen thousands of patients, I have never met a person who could not solve his or her own problems—no matter how overwhelming they seemed. My patients came to me because they did not know how to get a fresh perspective on themselves. I am sharing the techniques I developed to help my patients with you so that you can be your own healer. We all have latent powers to heal ourselves within.

To make a successful escape from tranquilizer dependency, you need to know what vitamins and minerals you need. Everyone should take a multiple vitamin and mineral supplement daily. The specific type is not particularly important. What is important is that the supplement be a normal part of your daily diet. It is meant to compensate for some of the nutritional deficiencies that are built into modern life, what with pollutants, denatured foods, and meals "on the run."

If you can find a tablet that doesn't contain copper, I recommend using that. Copper is an essential mineral, but we need only a trace of it. Taken in larger quantities, copper can trigger a minor depression in some people.

But the important thing is to take the vitamin and mineral supplement as part of your daily routine. You'll be glad you did.

4

Your First Day

But how do you do it? How do you wean yourself from tranquilizers? How do you wake up tomorrow morning and plan *your first day* of decreasing drug dependency?

The first step is to decide by how much you want to reduce your tranquilizer use, keeping in mind that your *daily* dosage for any given week may not be decreased by more than 5 mg if you are to avoid serious withdrawal complications. If you are currently taking as much as 30 mg per day of any tranquilizer, you probably will want to go for the maximum reduction (25 mg per day for each day of the first week, 20 mg per day for each day of the second week, and so forth). But if you have been taking a small dosage, such as 10 mg, you might want to reduce only to 8 mg per day for the first week, 6 mg per day for the second, and so forth.

Some tranquilizers come in dosages small enough for you to eliminate one pill per day. That would be the case if you have been taking six 5-mg tablets for your 30-mg dose. It doesn't always work out that neatly, however. For example, your doctor may have told you to take one 10-mg tablet each day. In that case, use a sharp knife to cut approximately one-fifth of the tablet. Throw this small piece into the toilet and take the remaining four-fifths (approximately 8 mg) as you normally would. But do throw that small piece away. You don't want to be tempted to take it later in the day during a period of stress. You don't need it, and though it does cost you money, it is a small price to pay for freedom from dependency on something your body doesn't need.

Plan your dosage so that the last dose of the day is your smallest, assuming you take the tranquilizer more than once a day. For example, if you were accustomed to taking 30 mg per day in 10-mg doses, you should now switch to taking 10 mg in the morning and 10 mg at midday, as always, and reduce the final dose to 5 mg. If you normally take your tranquilizer in a single dose, naturally you will take the reduced dose at that time.

The second step of your first day's plan involves the consumption of vitamins. Learning which vitamins to take when is going to require some effort on your part. For weeks, months, or possibly years you have let yourself be drug-dependent. If you are like many of my clients, you have seldom ventured out of your home without that reassuring bottle in your pocket. If you were troubled by the children, pained by a back injury, pressured by the boss, fighting with your lover or spouse, feeling stress from the rush-hour freeway traffic, or otherwise subjected to stress, you knew that the solution was always at hand in the form of a single, tidy pill. Then, gradually, you realized you had lost control. *You* were not coping with life; *your pills* were masking reality for you. *You* were not making decisions. *Your pills* were helping you avoid the decision-making process, letting you drift along without resolving anything.

Now you have decided to stop being pill-dependent. You are going to cut back. To do this, I am going to tell you to take *more* pills than you have ever taken before. Psychologically, this is hard.

The pills I am going to tell you to take are *vitamins*. Vitamins are organic molecules not made in the body that are required to sustain the normal metabolic process. Vitamins assist the body's processing of one's major nutrients, protein, fats, and carbohydrates. Certain vitamins participate in the formation of blood cells, hormones, nervous-system chemicals, and genetic material. Only Vitamin D is made organically in the body (from natural sunlight). Vitamins are the keys to your physical survival, mental alertness, and ability to function as a whole person.

The amount of vitamins you should take is determined by the amount of mental and physical stress you undergo. You are under mental stress in the first place to take tranquilizers. Tranquilizers, like antibiotics or any other kind of medication, leach essential nutrients from your system. Foreign substances demand extra vitamins for your body's metabolic processes to work. This creates a new physical stress.

Sugar is a classic example. Totally raw sugar cane found in the wild contains everything needed for proper metabolism. However, the moment it is refined (and even brown sugar is a refined sugar colored with molasses), the B complex vitamins are removed. This creates a serious problem most people never think about. Sugar cannot be metabolized by the body without Vitamin B complex. Since that B complex has been removed in the processing, it must be obtained from somewhere else in the body. Other food eaten during the same meal might have some, but that is needed for the metabolism of those other foods. Thus the body must rely on B complex that has been stored. Unfortunately, the body only stores excess vitamins A and D.

Lastly, the body in an anxiety state does not assimilate nutrients as efficiently as the stress-free body, thus dosages must be increased. But the eight fragile B vitamins and Vitamin C are not stored in the body so if your body is depleted of these vitamins, it has no source to tap except the vital store that the cells need for normal functioning. Eventually this leaves the cells deficient and results in disease. Heart disease can be a side effect of too much sugar, as can hypoglycemia, diabetes, problems with the pancreas, and many others.

If you have been putting sugar in your coffee or consuming sweets such as doughnuts and candy, the hidden sugar in most canned vegetables, condiments such as catsup, and even cigarettes (tobacco is sugar-cured and some sugar is inhaled with the smoke), you are probably deficient in Vitamin B complex. This deficiency results in low blood sugar, the symptoms of which are anxiety, nervousness, inability to handle pressure, and a sense of desolation and alienation. These symptoms may be the very ones for which you have been taking tranquilizers. This condition often goes unrecognized, and I will be placing emphasis on it in this book.

The longer food is out of the ground or off the tree, or picked preripened, the more it loses its vitamins and minerals. "Fresh" fruits and vegetables may be several weeks from the farm by the time you buy them. Frozen foods have an even more reduced nutritional value; and canned vegetables the least of all, because they have been cooked.

I'm not going to suggest that you eat only organic foods. I know our diets are going to contain some processed foods and chemical additives.

It is important to understand your body's optimum nutritional requirements, monitor your deficiencies, and then understand how to compensate for them. The nutrition section of this book tells you how to discover proper foods to address particular stress points. Especially while weaning yourself from tranquilizers, help your system in every way you can.

There is nothing wrong with taking vitamins. All excess vitamins are sloughed out in the urine except vitamins A, D, E, and K. Although Vitamin E is a fat-soluble vitamin that accumulates in the body, possible toxic effects of large doses have not yet been defined. However any dosage up to 1000 mg a day is not considered an overdose. As for Vitamin K, excessive use can also be toxic, but it is only available through prescription. You should limit your intake of Vitamin A and Vitamin D to the contents of a multiple vitamin/ mineral tablet. All the other vitamins cannot harm you in the quantities I recommend because they are water-soluble. If I say to start with 2500 mg (2.5 grams) of Vitamin C and you decide that 5000 mg are best for you, you can take it safely. If your body needs the 5000 mg, you will use it all. You should not relate the vitamins to the tranquilizers, sleeping pills, and other pharmaceuticals you are trying to eliminate from your normal day. A vitamin comes in pill form, but that is where the similarity ends.

Vitamins are the essential building blocks of life. They are the natural tools that will help you to live drug-free, happy, and serene. I am asking you take many vitamins to rid yourself of dependency on what might be just one tranquilizer or sleeping pill. You can't become addicted to vitamins. Taking several vitamins is a *positive step* in your life and *NOT* the substitution of one dependency for another. Remember, the higher doses are temporary means to get you through the withdrawal.

The basic vitamins with which you will start each day include Vitamin B complex "100" (100 mg of each of the B complex vitamins combined in a single pill), choline, pantothenic acid (all these are part of the B complex family even though the names are different), Vitamin C, niacinamide, Vitamin E. You will also take either dolomite (a mineral) or L-tryptophane, and zinc. And you should also take a daily multivitamin-mineral tablet.

In addition, many of my patients like to take a morning pep-up drink, because as a food supplement it goes right into their blood streams at the beginning of the day. The recipe is: 1 teaspoon brewer's yeast in either powder or flake form, 1 teaspoon protein powder, 1 teaspoon dry skim milk powder, and 1 teaspoon lecithin granules, blended with a glass of milk or tomato juice. Some people say that the yeast, though nutritional, causes mild nausea. They prefer to skip the drink and eat lecithin granules plain, a tablespoon at a time, three times a day. The lecithin granules are extremely valuable for the body and taste much like cashew nuts. One tablespoon of lecithin contains 500 milligrams of choline, that crucial ingredient for alleviating the withdrawal symptoms. The protein powder should be a specific type (though the brand does not matter). The label should tell you that it is 90 percent protein powder made from yeast and papaya enzymes. (Beware of protein powder made from chocolate.)

The other alternative to the morning beverage is to eat a tablespoon of lecithin granules combined with a tablespoon of bee-pollen pellets and 2 tablespoons of rice bran for fiber. This, like the drink, is optional. Only the vitamins and the three tablespoons of lecithin granules should be considered essential to the program.

Each of us is unique. Our bodies come in different sizes and shapes. We have varying heights and weights. We encounter different stress factors and deal with them in ways that might be simple for one person and overwhelming for another. As a psychotherapist, I am comfortable working eight or ten hours a day listening to the troubles of others, helping them to find new ways to view their problems and getting them to achieve an inner peace and understanding without drugs. However, I know a construction worker who spends his days high atop scaffoldings. He thinks the stress of what I do would drive him crazy, while I know I would never be able to handle the responsibilities and work pressures of high-rise construction. His stress areas and mine are different. Just as differences in our biochemistry and in our ability to handle stress vary widely, so will our requirements for nutrients. There is no uniform dosage. Both the construction worker and I follow the plan in this book, and it enables us to deal with our day without tranquilizers, sleeping pills, or antidepressants. I take more Vitamin C than he does, and he needs more Vitamin B complex than I do. We started with the same base of vitamins, then increased some and decreased others according to our individual mental and physical needs.

I recommend that you do the same. The vitamins you start on your first day are a base. You then modify your doses according to your mental and physical needs, include what you receive in the multiple vitamin-mineral tablet you take, plus what you get naturally from healthy food and sunshine.

Ideally, you should take your vitamins throughout the day after eating. If you can program yourself to do that, great! However, if you are like me and almost everyone I know, you will tend to forget to take your vitamins once you become too wrapped up in the tasks of the day. You may forget what you took and when you took it, a problem especially to be avoided at this critical time when you need to counter the stress of the chemicals from which you are trying to withdraw. This problem can be avoided if you take all your "basics" first thing in the morning. That's the reason I emphasize the morning drink.

Whether you take your vitamins in the morning or spread them throughout the day, they should include the following: a multiple vitamin and mineral tablet; 100 mg of zinc; 2500 mg of Vitamin C; 1000 mg of choline; 800 IU of Vitamin E if you are a man, or 600 IU if you are a woman; at least 500 mg of panthothenic acid (1000 mg if you have arthritis); 500 mg of Vitamin B_6; 1000 mg of Vitamin B_3 in the form of niacinamide; and four Vitamin B complex 100 pills. The latter is Vitamin B complex formulated to give you 100 mg of each of the B vitamins, not 100 mg of one, 50 mg of another, perhaps 15 mg of a third, and so forth. Check the label on this one carefully to make sure that is what you are getting. Different B vitamins cost varying sums to manufacture. Containers of B complex, actually one vitamin containing all the different B vitamins, are sometimes formulated for profit, not consumer need, and are topheavy with the B vitamins that are cheaper to manufacture. The label may say "stress formula" or "high potency," but the formulation is based on cost. You want to buy only the B complex that contains 100 mg of each.

Throughout the day there are going to be periods of stress when you may crave your tranquilizer. You can stop the craving by taking 500 mg or more of choline. You should also take 1000 mg of niacinamide and from 200 to 500 mg of pantothenic acid. These will give you a feeling of well-being—a godsend when you are facing the intense strain of getting off tranquilizers. You might keep a supply of these vitamins in your desk, your cupboard, or anywhere they are handy, using them as a constructive means of handling the stress. Take your vitamins after eating or have a glass of milk or an egg beforehand, to assure assimilation.

Nighttime may be the roughest period of the day for you. Sleep may not come easily. If you are spreading your tranquilizers throughout the day when you start this program, you will be cutting back this last dosage. If you have been taking a nightly sleeping pill too, you will not be reducing the amount of that pill until you are free from tranquilizers—at which time you will take an additional 1000 mg of niacinamide, additional pantothenic acid, and either dolomite or L-tryptophane as you wean yourself from sleeping pills.

L-tryptophane is an amino acid that induces sleep. It is released from milk when the milk is heated—which is the reason many people find a glass of warm milk a soporific.

L-tryptophane is available in tablet form; six to nine tablets should prove adequate. Unfortunately, it is expensive. You can substitute a low-cost calcium/magnesium pill known as dolomite. Dolomite must be taken in *double* the quantity of the L-tryptophane, but even at that rate it is relatively inexpensive. Dolomite is just calcium and magnesium as found in nature. It is as safe to take as vitamins. I will tell you more about it in the chapter on sleep.

This is the core of my program for freeing you from your tranquilizer addiction. To round it out, I am going to recommend some changes in your eating habits, a moderate exercise program, some relaxation techniques, and a healing way of talking out your problems.

Does the program really work? Consider Marilyn, a woman whose face is familiar to everyone who has ever passed a magazine stand. Marilyn (not her real name, of course) is one of our nation's most famous models. She is a beautiful young woman in her midtwenties, happily married, and has appeared on the covers of some of the most elegant fashion magazines.

When Marilyn stepped into my office, she looked twenty years over her age. Her face was lined, her eyes had a dull look, she was lethargic, her most animated action was lighting a cigarette—and puffing rapidly to get to the next one.

> Dr. Green, I feel so foolish being here. For years my doctor has said that tranquilizers are the answer to my problems, but now I'm afraid the tranquilizers have become my problem. I can't seem to do *anything* without them. But when I tried to quit them once, I've never been so sick in my life. I'm a model and I went to the shooting session shaking and nauseous. I blew two hours of work and God knows how many thousands of dollars for the photographer before I took one of the Valiums his secretary had to give me enough control to go on. I haven't been off tranquilizers since, but I know they aren't helping me. I'm not getting anywhere with my career. I'm not. . . .

At that point, Marilyn began sobbing. She was deeply upset and it took me several minutes before I could get her to tell me her story. At first I thought she was one of those women who develop an ambition twenty years later than is realistic, going off in their forties determined to pursue a career appropriate for someone more youthful. When I learned that Marilyn was twenty-three, I realized just what a toll her tranquilizer addiction had already taken.

> My whole world was shattered when I was sixteen. My father died and my mother remarried a man who had never had any children. He resented my presence around the house. He tried sending me away to school, but when that became too expensive, he wanted me to quit my education and get a job. We fought constantly, and my mother usually took his side. She told me she knew her new husband was in the wrong, but she also knew I was getting older and would be leaving home soon. Her new husband would be with her the rest of her life, so she felt she had to try and keep him happy even if it was at my expense. She said I should understand, but all I did was overeat and develop a skin condition. I became withdrawn and miserable.

Eventually Marilyn went to a doctor who prescribed tranquilizers. The doctor also suggested she get into some activity away from the house, and Marilyn ended up taking a modeling course in a fly-by-night school whose owner pretended this weeping woman, weighing 150 pounds and with blemished skin, could find work.

Marilyn fell in love with modeling but had the maturity to realize that she was being taken advantage of. She felt she had learned enough about the field and herself to lose weight, use makeup to hide her blemishes, and was able to obtain modeling assignments. This she did, trimming down to 112 pounds on her attractive 5-foot-10-inch frame.

Eventually Marilyn found her way to Europe and began modeling seriously. However, though she was developing her ability in the eyes of others, Marilyn still saw herself as a frightened, unloved, overweight lump dominated by a stepfather she hated and a weak mother. She always feared she wouldn't be good enough for a picture-taking session, so she fortified herself with Valium. She also ate irregularly to try to maintain her weight, and used thick makeup to hide increasingly serious skin problems that were aggravated from improper nutrition. She smoked heavily as a way of curbing her appetite, placing another strain on her nervous system.

Marilyn was fighting a battle against herself. She made her life all the harder. She was taking 30 mg of tranquilizers, chain-smoking, drinking too much coffee, and having one affair after another: "I wanted desperately for someone to love me. But I've never loved myself and I've never let myself get serious about someone. When I thought I was getting too involved, I ran from the relationship."

When I put Marilyn on my tranquilizer-withdrawal plan, I had no idea just how effective it could be. She seemed an extreme case and I had not realized until then how much chemical stress could alter someone's appearance.

The first week was difficult for Marilyn. She had trouble sleeping (a problem we will discuss in a later chapter) and she seemed to live on niacinamide and choline just before each photography session, when she felt the most stress. She wasn't under any greater stress than before, but now she was helping her system nutritionally with vitamins—instead of fleeing it through tranquilizers.

By the end of the second week, Marilyn had changed. She was down to 20 mg of her tranquilizer each day and regaining control of her emotions. She was eating more regularly, but the increased exercise and improved nutrition helped her metabolize and prevented weight gain. Yet the exercise only involved walking from studio to studio, distances she could cover in ten to fifteen minutes at a time. It was simple and did not disrupt her day as she had feared. She was also cutting back on her cigarettes, smoking now for the enjoyment she got from them rather than as a nervous habit.

It took Marilyn six weeks to get off tranquilizers and another three weeks to rid herself of the sleeping pills to which she was also addicted. Then she used the same methods to almost entirely eliminate cigarettes from her life, though she chose to continue smoking occasionally.

By the end of three months, Marilyn was physically transformed. The lines about her face were gone and her complexion was smooth and clear. She looked years younger—and far more beautiful.

Marilyn also experienced a dramatic change in her personal life. She met a successful lawyer and used the talking-it-out techniques in this book to get to know him at the same time she discovered herself. They fell in love and Marilyn felt no need to run from the relationship or worry about whether she was good enough for him. She had come to understand herself.

The change in attitude and appearance was accompanied by a change in bookings for Marilyn. Photographers who had worked with her for low-paying catalog work were suddenly demanding her for covers of major magazines. She appeared in all the leading high fashion magazines and told me she felt as though she had gotten "a second chance in life."

Today Marilyn is married and enjoying career success. She is under greater pressure than ever before, but she handles it with nutrition and exercise, not tranquilizers. She looks her age, and has found happiness she had never felt she deserved. And Marilyn accomplished all this by utilizing the techniques outlined in this book.

Frank was another of my patients who was heavily addicted to tranquilizers. Frank was a schoolteacher who took Valium initially as a muscle relaxer because of pain from a minor back injury. Then he discovered that as a side effect the drug reduced the pressures of teaching high school students. His doctor saw nothing wrong with letting him continue to have these positive benefits. By the time Frank came to me he had been a ten-year user of Valium. He was addicted and knew it, even though his doctor insisted that the dosage was safe.

"I feel like I'm completely falling apart," said Frank. "Even my marriage is in trouble because I always seem too tired to make love to my wife. When we do have relations, I'm never certain I'll get an erection, even though I used to be able to enjoy making love, sometimes as often as twice a day."

Frank had become concerned about the drugs. "I told my doctor I didn't want to take Valium any more so he prescribed Librium. I said that wasn't what I had in mind as a substitute, so he suggested Miltown. He offered me pills to fight pills and then had the nerve to say his wife has been on the drugs even longer than me, and she has no complaints. He couldn't think of anything but his damned pills and I know I've got to stop."

The problems Frank was having were typical of those many tranquilizer addicts have. Frank happened to be dependent on Valium, but Valium, though the most widely sold "minor" tranquilizer, is no different from any of the others in its effects. Impotence, difficulty in obtaining and maintaining an erection, is often related to long-term use of tranquilizers. Other difficulties patients have expressed to me include lack of memory and confused thinking. These do not happen in every case, but they do occur frequently enough for you to recognize them as some of the concerns that led you to read this book.

The program in this book has helped many of my patients over the years, and Frank was no exception. The nutritional deficiencies created by the stress of the tranquilizer were countered by the vitamins and diet. Frank got off drugs and also regained his sexual abilities. He improved his relationship with his wife by talking honestly and openly for the first time in years. Instead of running from his problems by taking a tranquilizer, he learned to handle stress through the alternatives in this book. When he no longer felt the need to flee, he also found that he could "talk it out," and this brought him closer together with the woman he had feared he might lose.

Users of certain medications such as Aventyl, Tofranil, and Librax as well as Valium may experience slight nausea as a side effect during the first three to five days of withdrawal. If you do, be assured that it is minor and will be temporary. It is the slight price you pay for the chance to live drug-free. The nausea will pass. Just remember that with such drugs, the nausea is caused from the toxic effect on your body chemistry during withdrawal, and not any problem with the plan.

This plan works. You are going to live tranquilizer-free no matter how many weeks, months, or years you have gone without ever being more than a few feet from your trusty bottle of blues or whites. You do not need tranquilizers. By following this plan, you will once again know the joy of living in control of your destiny. You will never regret the few short weeks necessary to achieve this end safely and effectively.

Don't look at this transition as a dread, horrible facing-up. It's not. It's a period of growth and liberation. As you feel the sharpening of your perceptions and the messages from your body, you are actually getting back in touch with the part of you that was numbed by tranquilizers. This book gives you the tools for growth as you say goodbye to tranquilizers forever.

5

Foods and Moods

It was one of those depressing November days that hints of a cold and miserable winter to come. The sky had been overcast all morning, and on the streets of New York drivers had turned their lights on by midafternoon. The temperature hovered near the freezing point and the wind whipped pedestrians as they hurried about their business.

The light in my office was subdued when Jack entered the room and the relative darkness seemed to upset him. "Why don't you turn on more lights in here?" he said, throwing the wall switch. "It's bad enough being so dark and dreary outside. Though I've got to admit this weather seems to fit the way my life has been going lately."

Jack sat down, struggling to get comfortable. He was obviously ill at ease and I waited for him to find the words to express himself. "I don't know what I'm doing here. You're the seventeenth psychotherapist I've seen and the only reason I came was because I've heard you don't believe in drugs except as a last resort. I don't know what you're going to tell me to take but I doubt that you'll come up with anything new. I've had Librium, Mellaril, Valium, Miltown, and God knows what else. None of them has helped. Nothing changes, except now I can't get off the tranquilizers, I can't solve my problems, and I'm screwed up worse than ever."

I asked Jack what seemed to be his problem.

What isn't? I guess the big thing is that I'm depressed all the time. I feel rotten and nobody can tell me why. One shrink said I'm depressed because I hate my father. Another shrink said I love my father but my depression comes from the fact that my father hated my mother. Only my father didn't hate my mother and even if he did, that would have been his problem, not mine.

And there's this headache. I guess I can count the number of times I've awakened without a headache on the fingers of one hand. I got one out in the wind out there. I had another one because you had the lights on low and now that they're up, I'm probably getting one from the brightness.

I could understand it if I was sick, but I'm healthy as a horse. I've been tested for high blood pressure, glaucoma, cancer, heart disease, emphysema, hardening of the arteries. My arms probably look like a heroin junkie's with all the things jabbed into me. But nobody has any answers. They just give me more blue pills, some yellow pills, a few white ones or whatever. I know I'm addicted to the tranquilizer I'm getting right now, I take way too much Darvon, and every night I can't seem to sleep without my Dalmane. I'm still depressed. I still get headaches and I don't know what to do. The last guy I saw said I was schizophrenic and wanted to switch me to Thorazine, but that didn't make much sense, either.

I had heard complaints concerning headaches and depression from others and the cause often turned out to be unrelated to the diagnosed illness.

"Tell me about yourself," I suggested. "Do you feel hungry when you wake up in the morning?"

"Hungry?" said Jack, surprised by the question. "I feel hungry all day. I go to bed hungry and I wake up hungry. But what does that have to do with my headaches and depression?"

Jack's problems sounded familiar. I had heard them from others on tranquilizers. I suspected that Jack's problem, the cause of the depression for which he had been given so many pharmaceuticals, was one common to a great many people. "How do you cope with that hunger?" I asked.

"Chocolate bars," said Jack. "I always carry a couple in my suit pocket. Instant energy, you know. Rush of sugar makes me feel better quickly so I can go on with my work. I'm an extremely busy executive and I find I function best by eating something every time I get a little hungry."

"What sort of food do you eat throughout the day?" I asked.

> Good food. I always have a great meal at night and I take what I can during the day. Usually I start with coffee and doughnuts in the morning for breakfast. That holds me until around eleven when I take one or two chocolate bars for a quick snack. That stops the shaking and the hunger until I can break for lunch.
>
> Lunch . . . well, I eat what I can. There's a sandwich joint near the office and either my secretary or I will grab something most days. It's a pretty good meal, though. A hamburger and Coke, maybe a couple of Danish or a piece of apple pie. It's quick but a lot of protein.
>
> About four in the afternoon somebody in the office goes down to the pastry shop and I get some cheesecake, maybe a little ice cream or something like that. It's not very big but it holds me.
>
> When I finally get home for dinner, I always have a good meal. Usually it's a little steak or fish and dishes with cream sauce. I loved creamed potatoes or French fries with my steak and I always have vegetables. Then for dessert I might have a piece of apple pie àla mode or some chocolate cake and a few cups of coffee. I might have some vodka and beer during the day as well. Not a whole lot—never more than five or six throughout the day and night if I stay up late watching television.

As I listened to Jack, I had a feeling I knew just what his problem might be. The tranquilizers and Darvon, the sleeping pills, and all the other medication he had been on were all meant to treat *symptoms*. The doctors had neither found nor treated the root cause that seemed so obvious. Jack, if my suspicions were confirmed by the medical testing I ordered for him, was a victim of hypoglycemia—low blood sugar.

Hypoglycemia is one of the most common sources of emotional problems in America today. It affects at least twenty million people. These are the individuals whose low blood sugar has been diagnosed. How many *undiagnosed* hypoglycemics may exist remains unknown. It is suspected that certain illnesses are influenced by low blood sugar. For example, Nobel Prize scientist Dr. Linus Pauling has speculated that at least half the individuals diagnosed as schizophrenic actually are affected by low blood sugar.

What are the symptoms of low blood sugar? As Jack was surprised to learn, they include headaches and depression. There may also be insomnia, difficulty in maintaining concentration, periodic confusion, restlessness, sweating, cold hands and feet, pain in the joints, over-reactivity, inability to handle stress—the complaints many of my patients had had when the doctors they consulted prescribed tranquilizers. Most alcoholics are hypoglycemics, yet some doctors prescribe tranquilizers when helping an alcoholic patient try to get off the bottle.

Hypoglycemia may lead to other ailments as well. Diabetes is the most common complication, but hypoglycemics may develop asthma, food allergies, coronary thrombosis, peptic ulcers, and rheumatic fever.

Many people spend their lives affected just by the hypoglycemia, reacting emotionally to it and being treated with tranquilizers, stimulants, and sleeping pills. Jack seemed to fall into this category when a change of diet would have been all that was necessary.

I arranged for Jack to take the Seale Harris test for hypoglycemia. This test, named for the doctor who invented it, determines how the body is handling glucose, commonly called blood sugar. It is a safe, simple procedure that proves conclusively whether or not a hypoglycemic condition exists. Currently it is the only effective test. Even routine tests for diabetes cannot be used to detect hypoglycemia. Though Jack's tests had never indicated a diabetic condition, he was surprised to discover that he did have hypoglycemia. Naturally he was angry that he had been given tranquilizers to alter his mood without anyone's having considered whether nutrition would have had the same effect—and cure his condition.

Jack was certain that being hypoglycemic meant no longer being able to enjoy life. But when I showed him some of the diet programs to correct it, he was greatly relieved.

Naturally, refined sugar had to be eliminated from his diet. Refined sugar rushes into the blood stream, tapping as much insulin from the pancreas as if the stomach had had a full meal. It forces the glucose level in blood to rise rapidly; the insulin then causes the glucose level to fall severely. This roller-coaster reaction results in overwhelming hunger, headaches, and any number of problems that many people solve by taking a candy bar or doughnut, or a tranquilizer, much as Jack handled his problem. Unfortunately the sweet food recreates the chain of events that caused the original headache. The rush of sugar followed by too much insulin results in yet another drop in blood sugar and yet another headache. It is a perpetual cycle for hypoglycemics.

This relentless cycle of hypoglycemia ends in one of two ways. If the victim learns what is wrong, as Jack did, a change in diet stops the problem immediately. It is an instant "cure" without medication or bad side effects. However, if the victim fails to face the problem, he or she eventually exhausts the pancreas' ability to make insulin. This results in a new illness called diabetes.

Sugar may be the cause of a second problem. In order for the sugar to be metabolized by the body, B complex vitamins must be obtained. These have to be "stolen" from other parts of the body, creating a general weakness and, in many cases, depression. Such mood changes disappear with the extra vitamins taken as a supplement or with the elimination of refined sugar from the diet, coupled with a supplement to rebuild your health.

"Do you mean to say that I have been a victim of what I eat all these years? I've become depressed, angry, and now a tranquilizer addict all because I ate the wrong foods?" asked Jack.

"Your medical reports indicate that," I told him. "Had your previous doctors done some simple testing instead of handing you a prescription for tranquilizers, you would be fine today."

"But they didn't, and I never thought such a problem was possible. I wanted that magic pill. I wanted an instant answer. And the tranquilizers did work. I felt calmer after I took them, even though I was always upset with the idea that I couldn't get through the day without my bottle of blues or yellows or whatever the tranquilizer of the week happened to be."

Many of my patients started on tranquilizers for the same reason. Hypoglycemia is one of the most common reasons adults have mood shifts that lead them to psychiatrists' offices. The patient assumes he or she can't cope without tranquilizers because the counseling usually only lessens the anxiety. Counseling and coming to an understanding of yourself are important, but they won't stop anxiety caused by diet.

The diet Jack began following eliminated refined sugar without eliminating the enjoyment of eating. (For some general guidelines about which foods to eat and which to avoid while following my program, see Appendix 2.)

I recommend dietary changes to all my patients when they are getting off tranquilizers, regardless of whether they have hypoglycemia or not. Take a close look at your diet with a view toward eliminating sugar, starchy foods, white rice, traditional candy, cakes, pies, doughnuts, cookies, sugared chewing gum, pizza, chocolate, alcoholic beverages, sugared soft drinks and colas, popcorn, catsup, potato chips, sweetened fruit juices, canned and frozen vegetables containing sugar (read the label; sugar is used in an astonishing range of products to alter the taste), and anything with corn syrup, maltose, sucrose, and dextrose—which are actually all the same as refined sugar to the body. You can have a vast variety of meat, cheese, fish, vegetables, desserts made without sugar and chocolate (carob brownies, for example), and whole-grain breads. You can enjoy the natural sweetness of fruits and the crunchy taste of nuts.

Why do I say that someone getting off tranquilizers should change the types of foods eaten? Because the stress that hypoglycemia causes for some people can add to everyone's anxiety. You take a tranquilizer because you are having difficulty dealing with temporary or long-term stress. Why continue a diet which can add to that stress when a slight modification during the time you are following my plan eliminates it? Why not substitute carob for chocolate, herbal tea or bouillon for coffee (caffeine also creates an adrenalin rush), and eliminate sugar so you can speed yourself toward your goal? And why not eat foods that haven't been processed or altered and reap the benefits of the vitamins and minerals needed to restore what the chemical tranquilizer has damaged?

In addition to the change in diet, I stressed the importance of vitamin supplements for Jack. These are important to understand, so let's look at them in detail.

Choline is one of the B complex vitamins. It is found in eggs, fish, peanuts, beef liver, soybeans. It is a major key to getting off tranquilizers without withdrawal problems.

Choline is probably one of the least known and most important aspects of the B complex vitamins. It is not included in many multivitamin tablets, but it is essential for the smooth working of the nervous system that affects your total ability to function. Reduction in choline is one of the side effects of tranquilizer use, so a choline supplement is the answer to handling the cravings of tranquilizer withdrawal.

Nerve cells are separated from one another by tiny gaps known as synapses. The nerve fluid, acetylcholine, transmits nerve impulses across the gaps. If a truck is bearing down upon you as you cross the street, your brain needs to tell the muscles in your legs to work so that you can run from the danger. This signal to your leg muscles travels from nerve cell to nerve cell in a microsecond, enabling you to flee. However, when the synapses are damaged in some way and you have not taken enough choline to compensate, your body moves more slowly. In the case of the truck, you may be injured or killed. In a more ordinary situation, you may tire easily, have difficulty studying or thinking, or otherwise not find the ability to function as fully as you did before. Endorphin, a natural pain reliever in the brain, produces a morphinelike substance. Tranquilizers block the manufacture of endorphin.

There are two ways in which choline is essential when getting off tranquilizers. The first is in eliminating the cravings that come from withdrawal. Every time you crave a tranquilizer, take choline in quantities of around 1000 mg or more (at least 15 grains if bought in the 7.5-grain size commonly available). Take as much as you need until the cravings stop, even if you boost this intake to several thousand milligrams. As you have seen, you cannot overdose on a vitamin (except A or D) in a way that is physically harmful.

The second use of choline is to combat the affliction known as tardive dyskinesia, literally, "acute abnormal movements." It is a disease of the back rooms of mental hospitals where long-term patients receiving strong tranquilizers and antipsychotic drugs are kept. Their nerve synapses are burned out, and the patients develop incurable tics and aberrations in their physical movements. Their heads twitch, their tongues move in odd ways, they walk with jerks of their upper body. Such people remain that way for the rest of their lives, hidden away in the hospitals. Sometimes they become mentally healthy but have been on the drugs just long enough to develop a minor tic. They return to the general public and have to adapt to living with this freakish disability.

It is known that individual reactions to major tranquilizers vary greatly. Some people develop minor symptoms of tardive dyskinesia immediately. In others, the symptoms may not be apparent for years.

Today, we are discovering that increasing numbers of people taking "minor" tranquilizers for long periods experience some of these same side effects. I have seen them in my office.

When the client follows my plan for getting off tranquilizers, the tardive dyskinesia symptoms disappear. The heavy choline use stops the tics and odd movements—it serves as the wonder vitamin to restore normal nerve and body functions. (Choline has in fact been documented by Dr. Richard J. Wurtman in a recent paper in the *New England Journal of Medicine* as being beneficial in treating tardive dyskinesia.)

Choline has many other beneficial uses. My tranquilizer clients include the elderly, declared senile by their families and sometimes by their doctors. These individuals have not suffered physical damage which would affect the mind, such as a stroke. Instead, they have developed problems related to diet and nutrition. They are deficient in the B complex vitamins, of which choline is one. When they changed their eating habits and took heavy doses of choline and other vitamins and minerals they freed themselves of tranquilizer addiction, and simultaneously cured their senility. Their "senility" was actually a form of malnutrition.

A diet deficient in choline affects the arteries of the heart, the aorta, and other critical areas. A lack of choline can lead to hardening of the arteries and damage to the liver and kidneys.

Choline has been used to treat hepatitis, hypothyroid conditions, and numerous other problems. It is thus a key health factor in addition to its effect on the nerves. Because even minor tranquilizer use reduces the amount of choline available to the body and leads to problems that choline can solve, I stress it as an essential factor in getting off the tranquilizers.

Many patients tell me that their doctors first started them on tranquilizers as a means of coping with high blood pressure. "I was twenty-five at the time," said Maureen, an attractive blond in her early thirties. "I had had a routine physical examination and the doctor discovered my blood pressure was elevated. He said I should take tranquilizers to calm me when I was in periods of stress and that would ease the problem."

Maureen worked in a department store as a sales clerk at the time. It was in the middle of December and the Christmas rush.

I was selling dresses and that year it seemed like everyone was buying clothing for the holiday. The store was open forever and I was always so exhausted that I would drop into bed the moment I got home. Breakfast was whatever I could grab at a doughnut shop and lunch wasn't much better—when I could take it. Usually I worked through my break and somebody would sneak me a sandwich and coffee midafternoon. I'd load the coffee with sugar to keep me going, eventually drinking it cold if somebody came to buy something before I was done.

The pressures continued the same way. We had the after-Christmas sales and then I got a promotion. I was trying to prove my value to the store and I kept putting in more and more hours as I went to higher positions. Eventually I was the fashion director and my eating habits hadn't changed.

I got married when I was thirty-one, and by then I was really hooked on tranquilizers. My husband was equally career-oriented, but we told ourselves that we compensated for our nutritional problems by eating properly every Sunday. That was our day together and we would stay in bed until noon, read the paper, and cook fantastic dinners. We'd go to little neighborhood stores to get the freshest fruit and vegetables, then go to a butcher whose shop was open. We pretended we lived in Europe and did this every Sunday. We gorged ourselves on the finest foods we could buy and tried to convince ourselves that we made up for all the junk food our schedules forced us to consume all week.

The trouble was that my blood pressure never got any better and my tranquilizer use got worse. I went from 5 milligrams two or three times a week to as much as double that amount three times a day. I also began having other ailments that seemed all wrong for someone so young. Yet my doctor just handed me the tranquilizer prescriptions. He never questioned my nutrition or living patterns.

When Maureen went on my plan for getting off tranquilizers, she immediately changed her eating habits. She arose half an hour early and made herself an egg, or ate some cheese, or fish. She also had fruit, whole-wheat bread, and a small amount of butter. She avoided sugar and switched to decaffeinated coffee. She worried that the lack of caffeine and sugar would keep her from having energy at work but she soon discovered that the natural release of energy from the proper food actually made her more productive than when she was gulping her coffee on the way to work. If she took a break during the morning, it was for grapefruit juice, nuts, and/or cheese.

Maureen still felt guilty about going to lunch, but I persuaded her to take control of what she ate. She felt embarrassed at work because she wasn't eating the same cafeteria food the others were. I showed her who could bring a sandwich with lettuce, tomato, whole-wheat bread, and cheese, meat, or fish. She could use a plastic container to bring a large salad and utilize safflower oil and vinegar or lemon juice on it. The salad could have raw vegetables, cheese, lettuce, and other whole foods. It was rich in choline (eggs, nuts, and so forth), and her meals were supplemented with the vitamins stressed in the preceding chapter.

Maureen withdrew from tranquilizers slowly, taking almost two months to be chemically free. However, the increase in choline through proper diet and the taking of supplements began to yield positive results in just three weeks. Her blood pressure was lowered for the first time in more than eight years. She was under just as much job stress as ever, but her altered lifestyle brought her peace and well-being and physical health.

The problem Maureen faced was in her food attitude; she felt anything sold as food must be nutritious. Most of us have been led to believe that if we eat foods from the protein, fat, and carbohydrate families, we are well nourished. This does not take into account the *processing* of those foods or their freshness. However, if you are discriminating you can get proper nourishment from many commercial foods.

Whole-wheat and whole-rye bread is far better than white bread made with bleached flour.

Too many doctors forget that stress is relative to the individual's threshold to endure it. Sheila, one of my clients, is a successful stockbroker who trades thousands of shares of stock at a time. She is responsible for advising people on the best way to invest millions of dollars. The work is exciting to her and she thrives on it. But it might be overwhelming to her medical doctor. Being human, when he sees a problem, he projects his own ideas of how much stress someone else must feel. It's hardly surprising that he projects a need for tranquilizers for Sheila.

Sheila didn't find the stress in her job negative. She trusted her physician's interpretation and used his prescriptions for Valium and Librium. She never realized what new problems she would have with the tranquilizers.

Most of us experience stress in ways more subtle than we realize. Certainly we face it on the job. There are overwhelming days no matter what we do. We can love our work and still let it get the best of us.

Other forms of stress are less obvious. There is the stress of our home life, living with another person, commuting to work, and the like. However, there is also chemical stress caused by processed foods, refined sugar, the drugs we take, especially the tranquilizers, smoking, air pollutants, and so on. Most of these rob our bodies of the B complex vitamins, including choline, and the other nutrients already mentioned.

In women, vitamin B_6 plays an important role in helping maintain hormonal balance and easing difficulties associated with menstruation.

Perhaps the most important role of vitamin B_6 in the eyes of women who are taking birth-control pills is that it combats the depression for which tranquilizers or stimulants are often prescribed. Many women have side effects from birth-control pills that they attribute to other factors. They become irritable, dissatisfied with their work or personal relationships (though not for any reason they can pinpoint), depressed, and otherwise troubled. Many are tired and seem to have a reduced sex drive. What they fail to realize is that they are simply experiencing a B_6 deficiency.

Pantothenic acid has often been called the antistress vitamin. It is one of the most readily destroyed vitamins in any food processing, so most of us are not able to get an adequate amount in our diet. We must have a supplement and that supplement can work what seems like miracles.

Take the case of Peter. Peter was a mechanic who was plagued with arthritis. He first started taking tranquilizers as a muscle relaxant for occasional joint discomfort. As the years passed and the pain increased, so did his dosage.

"There's nothing we can do except treat the symptoms," doctors told him repeatedly. "The tranquilizer you are taking is a mild one. Long-term use is not desirable with any drug unless the circumstances of a client warrant. But in your case, the pain is intense enough that there is no reason for you to be worried about constantly refilling the prescription. A few months or a few years on Valium will not effect you adversely in any way."

"They lied to me, Dr. Green," said Peter. "I don't mean they deliberately tried to get me hooked on this stuff. They said it was harmless and I think they believed that. Now I'm hooked and even though I know your plan works, I've still got the hell of arthritis. Every time the boss or some customer yells, the pain gets worse. I'm under stress a lot and I'm scared about how much hurting I'll have to do after I get off the tranquilizers. I guess it's better to suffer that way than with the medication, but, still, I wonder. Life sure isn't fair sometimes."

"Nonsense," I told Peter. "Life can be wonderful. It's all in how we face it and one way I want you to face it is with an increase in the B complex vitamin known as pantothenic acid."

Studies of arthritic patients show that they are deficient in pantothenic acid. Increasing the amount of pantothenic acid has been known to arrest the arthritis completely and eliminate the problems that cause severe pain. Taking pantothenic acid to counter moments of stress in addition to adding this supplement to your regular diet can do far more than any tranquilizer ever created.

How much pantothenic acid should you take? For arthritics, 900 to 1000 mg a day. Some have been cured and several have the blood-test results to prove it.

Some of my clients had been given tranquilizers because they ground their teeth. Others had had muscle cramps or general "aches and pains." In most cases, a change in pantothenic acid intake was the answer.

You should be taking pantothenic acid supplements as discussed in the preceding chapter. But, there are also foods you can eat which increase the pantothenic acid content of your body. These include eggs, peanuts, soybeans, sunflower seeds, wheat bran, liver, heart, and kidney. Sunflower seeds are a major source of pantothenic acid as well as a delightful midday snack anyone can carry in a pocket or purse. Remember that altering your lifestyle to lead a drug-free existence does not mean that living is going to be dull and eating uninteresting. The best way to live is with more energy and greater pleasure.

Niacinamide does all sorts of things besides act as a tranquilizer. It dilates the blood vessels and thus improves circulation. This is important not only for the aging. It also helps speed other nutrients through the body, since the flow of blood is improved.

Niacinamide can reduce the cholesterol level of the blood stream. Large doses of niacinamide have in many dramatic cases caused the symptoms of schizophrenia to disappear. It helps allay one's craving for alcohol, and in large doses helps with the detoxification process. In addition it changes adrenalin, a major stress factor, into adrenochrome, a harmless chemical which no longer serves as a stimulant.

Tranquilizer users with poor diets frequently carry the visible signs of their need for niacinamide. Their skin can be blotchy and acne may be unusually bad. They may also have diarrhea, and problems with the mind such as impaired memory and difficulty thinking. In the extreme, someone who has little or no niacinamide will develop the disease pellagra. Often this is confused for senility in the elderly and people die tragically for want of the vitamin. Since they become addled and noisy during the period of suffering, more tranquilizers are prescribed. The tragedy of many nursing homes is that people are treated as though it is possible to have a tranquilizer deficiency and not a nutritional deficiency.

Many doctors will say that I am getting overly concerned about niacinamide deficiency. They point out that pellagra almost always occurs in extreme poverty areas. Most people get enough of the vitamin in their diets to compensate for their needs. Actually, this is only partially correct.

Pellagra is usually a disease of the poor, particularly in cultures that subsist primarily on corn. Corn does not contain vitamin B_3, so people who rely on the grain as their mainstay are deficient. There is, however, a much milder form known as subclinical pellagra. Subclinical pellagra occurs when niacinamide is available, but in insufficient amounts. This is a frequent cause of what is diagnosed as senility in the elderly.

A man I'll call Osgood was so sick that I had to see him in his home. He was in his seventies and had been active all his life. He was a professor of zoology, an author of numerous textbooks, and had been happily married for fifty years. He and his wife had been high school sweethearts and had stayed lovers until her death three years earlier. They had traveled the world and their hobby had been exploring the trails of the national parks around the country. When Osgood's wife died, his life changed. He became depressed, stopped eating properly, and eventually became a senile recluse. His family felt he belonged in a nursing home.

I was summoned to Osgood's home by his granddaughter, a young woman who had heard me talk about tranquilizer addiction and how the elderly often start on tranquilizers because of misdiagnosed diet problems. She told me that her grandfather had shown all the classic signs of senility only months after his wife died. He had blotchy skin, diarrhea, and what seemed to be emotional instability. Sometimes he would rant irrationally and at other times he would become depressed. The doctor put him on tranquilizers and that seemed to make him worse. When Osgood's granddaughter visited him, she realized that he had been eating a poor diet comprised of fast food purchased from a nearby drive-in and whatever packaged goods he felt like buying. Everything was heavily processed and sugared. She was convinced that either diet was the problem or contributed to it.

I put Osgood on my plan, stressing niacinamide. I agreed that diet was at least a contributing factor with his troubles and felt that he might be experiencing subclinical pellagra. The latter was never conclusively diagnosed by the doctor who had been prescribing the tranquilizers, but that did not matter. Within a few weeks of taking niacinamide and the other nutrients in my plan, there was a marked change in Osgood. Instead of sitting most of the day, he was hiking the streets of his neighborhood, greeting everyone with a smile on his face even during the worst weather. His mind became clear and he started writing again. His skin blotches faded and he returned to full health. The tranquilizer use was eliminated and the man reached a state where he could enjoy his retirement.

> It was my own fault, Dr. Green [Osgood later told me]. When Emma died I just didn't care about myself. I ate because I knew I had to, but I didn't have the heart to really go much beyond survival. Emma was a gourmet cook and we had dined in unusual restaurants around the world. I knew I could never match her skills and I didn't really care to try and learn even simple recipes. I ate junk food and I knew it but I never thought it could be so destructive for me. What scares me all the more is the fact that if my children had put me in a nursing home, the quality of care probably would not have countered all the problems I created for myself.
>
> I don't blame my children or think my granddaughter was so special for fighting the decision of

the others, though. I think I would have come to the same conclusion myself. Their father must have seemed to be slipping fast in their eyes and a nursing home would provide the increasing medical care they must have been certain I would need. I would have done the same to my own father, not having known what I know now. Your plan has given me a second life.

That was ten years ago. Osgood is less active today and has moved into a retirement community that has both apartments and medical-care facilities. He has his own apartment and continues to meet deadlines for more books than he ever thought he could write. His body is wearing out but he is approaching ninety with a clear mind and the vigor of a much younger man. Most important, he is not taking tranquilizers of any kind and is constantly hounding the dietician for the center to improve the nutritional quality of the meals. Fruit, not cookies, forms the midday snack for the people there, and brown rice, not processed white rice, is used in cooking. The costs have gone up for the people who stay there but their health is much better, and they spend less for medical treatment.

What are the sources for niacinamide? Among them are sunflower seeds, tunafish, halibut, chicken, turkey (white meat for both), liver, ham, peas, peanuts, brewer's yeast.

Vitamin C may be the most important vitamin for your health. It is a major factor in your ability to deal with stress. No matter what pressures you encounter, Vitamin C will be called upon to play a role in handling them. Vitamin C is also widely believed to be a natural antibiotic. Although it remains controversial, some studies have shown Vitamin C to be a major factor in fighting arthritis, and possibly cancer, blood problems, and other ailments. But the precise role of Vitamin C remains a matter of controversy, and much research remains to be done.

Remember that the body must treat *all* chemicals as if they were poisonous. The tranquilizers you take are battled internally at the same time they induce their calmative effect. The "war" being waged entails the depletion of Vitamin C. This stress erodes your health all the more. Thus the doses of Vitamin C I recommend will not only help you deal with the tranquilizers while you are slowly withdrawing in stages, but also help you counter the stress of the chemicals still remaining in your body.

You have probably been your body's worst enemy in the past, so this will be a major change in your future life without tranquilizers. By following the plan discussed in this book, you will become your body's friend.

Now let's explore other aspects of the plan which will help you do that.

6

Sleep,
the Magic Balm,
Can Be Naturally Yours

When the tall, distinguished-looking man came into my office complaining of sleep problems, I must say I was surprised. His picture had just appeared in *The New York Times* and the accompanying story led me to believe that he was one man who should be on top of the world.

Matthew is one of the nation's most successful songwriters. His songs have been performed and recorded by the best rock and pop artists. He is wealthy, respected, and at the very top of his profession. His clothing bore the stamp of Europe's finest custom tailors. The sports car he parked outside my office cost more than most people spend for their homes. Everything about him smacked of success and a carefree existence.

"Dr. Green, I'm miserable," said Matthew. "I haven't slept well in years. I take Quaaludes, Librium, and have tried just about everything else on the market. My doctor keeps insisting that he knows every prescription he gives me and that there's no danger, but lately, I don't believe he's right. I'm not getting adequate rest and sometimes I feel as though I'm becoming forgetful. I'm scared of what's happening to me."

I took a close look at Matthew. His eyes were slightly swollen. Lack of sleep had etched lines into his face. His fingers drummed the table. He looked like the perfect specimen for a "before" picture in a pharmaceutical company's advertisement for the latest tranquilizer. Like Janine, Matthew was a cross-addict—someone who had become dependent on tranquilizers as well as sleeping pills.

Matthew's problem started while he was in school. He was studying music during the day, then working as an assistant to an arranger from the moment his classes were done until well into the evening, after which he did personal projects. With school, the job, and his own efforts to work on his own songs that later proved to be his earliest award-winning accomplishments, Matthew was lucky to be able to sleep five or six hours a night. He found himself grabbing fast naps whenever he could, but he lived a life that did not allow for a consistent schedule. He slept when either exhaustion or a few free moments made all else impossible.

Eventually Matthew began to freelance on his own. He was one step ahead of the trends, constantly after a new and different sound that, at the time, wasn't what any of the big stars wanted. He had to divide his time so the bulk of it was spent handling conventional arrangements with the rest spent doing the jazz-oriented work that, today, has made him famous. Again his life was paced so that sleep was less than ideal.

Finally things began to change. Matthew discovered that singers were getting interested in his style. He also discovered that he had need for more intense personal relationships than just his few assistants. He met a rising executive in one of the record companies that recorded a friend of his. She was a beautiful, intelligent financial expert whose love of jazz and rock matched his own. She shared his drives and ambitions and understood his erratic hours. She also presented a stability that he had never known. They began dating and eventually decided to marry.

My life should have been perfect. All my dreams were being achieved. I was actually getting paid to let my mind run free and write for top people who wanted something new. I had found the perfect wife and we moved into a large home in upstate New York. We maintained a penthouse apartment in Manhattan and another apartment on the West Coast.

The problem was that my irregular living and sleeping habits over the years had made it impossible for me to rest at night. I kept finding myself leaving my wife's side at three in the morning to go to the piano and try something out. I couldn't seem to relax. I couldn't seem to get the rest I needed. I was terribly tense, and finally I went to see a doctor.

The doctor insisted that all I needed was a sleeping pill to help me rest. He tried me on what he said was a mild barbiturate, and it did knock me out. I spent more time asleep than ever before and each morning I awakened thinking I should feel wonderful. The problem was that I didn't even feel truly rested, I felt as if I had a slight hangover. I was drowsy during the day. I had to take a few cups of coffee to get going and clear my head.

I complained about what was happening and the doctor began experimenting with me. We tried other sleeping pills and tranquilizers. The doctor felt that my profession had exceedingly high stress and that perhaps Miltown or Valium would help. However, everything seemed to get worse.

Now things are out of hand. I'm barely sleeping at all, even though I take Quaaludes at night and Librium during the day to try and keep myself calmer I'm having trouble working, though so far it's not serious. It's just that I know I'm heading for trouble and I've got to find a way to live without sleeping pills.

Difficulty sleeping is one of the leading reasons many millions of Americans are abusing both sleeping pills and tranquilizers. Yet the greatest tragedy is that chemically induced sleep, whether with Quaaludes, Dalmane, Tuinal, or anything else, is not restful sleep.

Sleeping pills make the adrenals work and raise blood sugar. Any drug that interferes with sleep, which is the only time the adrenals are allowed to rest, puts hardship on the adrenals as they continue releasing sugar all night.

During natural sleep we pass through four levels. Initially, there is a floating sensation when you are first drifting off and still have difficulty telling what is real and what isn't. Progressively, as sleep becomes deeper and more intense, you reach the deepest level—where true rest occurs. This is the healing sleep, the helping sleep, the sleep that results in total relaxation. Once you have reached this level, you can be certain you will awaken rested and clear-headed. It is the sleep we all crave because it erases the cares of the day and lets our minds lie fallow, so that when we awaken we have the emotional strength to face the coming day.

Sleeping pills and tranquilizers induce sleep that falls short of our body's needs. The way the body reacts to the stress of the chemistry of a pill prevents our reaching that deepest level of sleep. We remain unconscious but not rested, and it is the need for rest that drives us to the pill in the first place.

I am *not* saying that pharmaceutical companies are trying to poison us. The drugs they create are meant to serve constructive purposes. But, our bodies were designed to function by ingesting protein, vegetables, fruits, vitamins, and other naturally available nutrients. Unrelated chemicals such as those found in prescription drugs do help alter our bodily functions. A tranquilizer can give you a sense of being calm at times. A sleeping pill can render you unconscious. But in the final analysis, sleeping pills and tranquilizers deal with symptoms, in this case insomnia and restlessness, and not the root causes of the lack of sleep.

Sleep is affected by any number of stress factors. Matthew had the problem of irregular working and sleeping habits. There was no consistent time when he could get to bed (sleep is easiest to obtain when we develop a reasonably consistent schedule). We may find ourselves sleepy when we need to work and with a fresh flow of adrenalin keeping us alert when we finally have the chance to drop off for a few hours.

Other problems with sleep are numerous. Sometimes we are faced with noisy neighbors. Having to listen to the overloud stereo, or the argument of the couple whose suite is directly above us, keeps us from drifting into the sleep we crave.

Insomnia is caused by various stresses. Perhaps the cause of stress is eating the wrong foods. A pepperoni pizza accompanied by garlic bread, beer, and a quantity of pickles is not likely to help induce sleep!

Environmental stress can come in several forms. There are the neighbors, of course, but also air pollutants, street noises, and numerous other factors. How these affect your sleep will vary not only with the environment you live in but with the type of person you are.

Insomnia is frequently caused by a vitamin or mineral shortage. A niacinamide deficiency, for example, can result in anxiety that prevents sleep. Some researchers now indicate that so-called coffee nerves, which keep people awake at night, are actually the result of a vitamin B_1 deficiency. Taking an additional 100-mg tablet of vitamin B_1 is better than any sleeping pill under such conditions. A thousand milligrams of inositol is an excellent sleeping aid. Leg cramps, particularly in the elderly, can interfere with sleep. This is frequently due to a magnesium deficiency, which can be easily corrected with magnesium tablets. I recommend 500 mg before going to bed.

A doctor usually feels pressured into prescribing sleeping pills for patients who can't sleep. The medication may indeed induce sleep, but it doesn't address the root problem. A sleeping pill is not going to solve a vitamin deficiency.

How can a sleeping pill deprive you of rest? We have already seen that sleeping pills prevent you from reaching what is known as the REM level of sleep. This is the deepest sleep, the level where you have what is known as Rapid Eye Movement. It is the level of true rest and, unless it is achieved, you cannot function effectively the next day. Your time in bed is not much more beneficial than if you had lain awake. Anxiety continues and compounds itself, encouraging you to continue with the sleeping pills, tranquilizer, or both even though they are not doing you any good.

A second form of chemical stress comes from the side

effects of the sleeping medications themselves, side effects frequently not reported to the doctors. For example, the manufacturer of Quaaludes warns that among the side effects are restlessness and anxiety—the very conditions for which the drug might be prescribed. Even more common are feelings of fatigue, headache, and hangover, again all problems for which you wanted a good night's sleep. Unfortunately, instead of blaming the drug reaction, most people feel they must continue the drug or even increase the dosage to address the problem. They fail to realize that they might be fine without the drug and troubled with it.

What about some of the other common products on the market? Dalmane can cause nervousness, apprehension, talkativeness, headache. Such side effects can create a vicious circle. You have trouble sleeping one night because you are nervous about a test in school or a meeting with your supervisor at work. You take a Dalmane to sleep, then conceivably awaken even more nervous because you now have both the original concern unresolved plus a side effect from the drug. You might take another Dalmane or induce your doctor to give you a stronger prescription and the problems continue.

Butisol sodium (Buticaps in capsule form) is another popular sleeping pill. Common reactions include a hangover feeling and drowsiness, both of which ensure that you will want to get a better sleep the next night.

Nembutal creates problems ranging from drowsiness to extreme excitability when you react to it. The drug is also addictive if taken too frequently and the warning to physicians includes a note that *gradual* withdrawal is essential.

On and on it goes. No matter what sleeping medication you mention, a careful check of some of the potential side effects will probably be enough to keep you awake at night. The body consistently reacts to these drugs by trying to fight them and this results in unconsciousness but not the achievment of vital REM sleep. More important, the longer such drugs are taken, the worse the side effects, including some of the problems for which the drugs were prescribed in the first place.

Medical doctors are often pressured by their patients to prescribe sleeping pills, especially by patients who feel these drugs have special powers. One of my clients was a young "swinger" whose life seemed to revolve around the Manhattan discos and nightclubs. He had an excellent job with an advertising agency and an independent income as well. His life was centered around sensuous pleasure and he heard that Quaaludes, in addition to being a sleeping pill, made an excellent aphrodisiac. By the time he realized that the pill would not make him a perpetual sex machine, he was addicted. He bought "ludes" on the black market in the nightclubs where they were readily available to anyone who could pay the price. No doctor was involved and no pharmaceutical company ever misled him. However, this did not make getting off the sleeping medication any easier. Even sadder is the fact that I have had a number of my patients come to me addicted to Quaaludes, though their physician-monitored dosage seemed proper.

The key to conquering sleeping problems is to reduce your stress level. Part of this means eliminating the chemical stress of the sleeping pills you are now taking. However, like the tranquilizer withdrawal, sleeping-pill withdrawal can lead to all manner of complications. You can have increased anxiety, much greater difficulty sleeping, resulting in emotional upset.

Sleeping pills, like tranquilizers, must be stopped very slowly. If you or someone you know is taking both types of pills, it is best to withdraw from just one at a time. First follow the plan to eliminate tranquilizers from your life, then continue with the identical plan for the sleeping pills. The entire process may take three to six weeks longer than withdrawing from just the single drug.

We have already seen that there are vitamins to duplicate the effect of tranquilizers. Some of these, such as niacinamide, can help induce sleep as well. This is because they relieve so much internal stress that you can relax without lying in bed, thinking of the problems of the day.

There are also two unique natural, problem-free counters

to sleeping pills. These are sold under the names L-tryptophane (or just tryptophane) and dolomite.

Remember when you were a small child and your grandfather had trouble sleeping? Grandmother might have given him a glass of warm milk just before bedtime. He would sip the contents and soon relax enough so that his snoring seemed to rattle the shutters of the house.

Perhaps you never thought much of the folk medicine represented by that glass of warm milk. However, over the many generations during which such a remedy has been used, doctors have noticed that it consistently worked. They were not certain if it was what was known as the placebo effect or if it had real value.

At an international conference on sleep in Edinburgh in 1974 it was disclosed that researchers had isolated an amino acid with fascinating properties. In effect, they had discovered why warm milk acts as a natural sedative. When the milk is warmed, an amino acid called L-tryptophane is released into the body.

Subsequently, a way was found to separate the tryptophane so that the amino acid could be consumed in tablet form. L-tryptophane is now packaged by a large number of manufacturers and sold in health food stores and other locations. You can buy it, take three to six tablets before retiring, and become as relaxed as if you had taken a sleeping pill. More important, when you lose consciousness, your body sinks into the all-essential REM sleep. You get the rest you need and you break the hold of insomnia.

Dolomite is a naturally occurring combination of the minerals calcium and magnesium, which are essential to the body. Trace amounts of lead, aluminum, and arsenic have been found in dolomite, creating a potential hazard in prolonged use, but not in sporadic and temporary use.

Dolomite is inexpensive. A good supply costs just a couple of dollars. L-tryptophane is new and, because of the involved process for obtaining the amino acid, can be quite expensive—eight dollars for just thirty tablets in some stores.

L-tryptophane also has a minor side effect in some people. It makes them nauseated, which some people experience when drinking milk.

Most of my clients find that they need one-third to one-half the L-tryptophane that they do dolomite. If they need six L-tryptophane tablets to drift naturally to sleep during the withdrawal period, they might find they need a dozen dolomite. Another alternative is a combination of two parts calcium to one part magnesium; for example, 1000 mg calcium and 500 mg magnesium.

Unless you want to try L-tryptophane, I suggest that you take dolomite if you have trouble sleeping during the withdrawal stage. Start with nine and take three more every twenty or thirty minutes if you remain restless. Usually a total of twelve to fifteen will be all you need to drift into a natural sleep. Patients who are highly agitated at bedtime often take from 1000 to 2000 mg of niacinamide as well. This is in addition to what you are taking to handle the withdrawal during the course of the normal day. I advise you to wash it down with some of that warm milk.

There are other ways to relax in addition to the taking of dolomite and L-tryptophane. One is through a type of meditation called fractional relaxation, which I discuss in the next chapter. Another, of course, is sex.

Sexual relations can be the most pleasant way to prepare for a good night's sleep. The loving, sharing, and sensuous pleasure of the relations causes you to forget the cares of the day. You focus only on your partner, sleep coming quickly and easily when you are done. It is conceivable that by following this plan and reaching for the person you love rather than a pharmaceutical, withdrawal from your addiction will also result in a closer relationship than ever before.

Matthew's problems all began with irregular sleeping habits and too little time in bed. He chose to use a pharmaceutical to handle his need for sleep and then gradually became dependent on it. Eventually he utilized my plan to free himself of both sleeping pills and tranquilizers.

Matthew did have one problem typical of everyone withdrawing from sleeping pills—and, to a lesser degree, from tranquilizers. There is going to be a period of from one to three days when your sleep may be less than you would like. You will sleep. That won't be the problem. You may have to use rather large quantities of dolomite or L-tryptophane in order to rest fully, but sleep will come, and it will be the effective REM sleep. However, during the first three days your sleep may not last as long as you would like. There is nothing wrong with this, and it does not mean that the program is failing. You will not have anxiety because your body is being calmed by the vitamins. However, you may sleep less than the number of hours to which you are normally accustomed.

Keep in mind that the temporary loss of sleep is not serious. It is part of the transition phase of getting off the drugs. Dolomite or L-tryptophane will help you achieve the REM level, and the vitamins I've recommended will keep you calm. Be patient, and enjoy the drug-free sleep you are newly experiencing.

Remember, the natural state of your body is healthy and drug-free. By combining the various aspects of this plan, nutrition, exercise, controlled relaxation, and the method of talking out your problems discussed in Chapter 8, you will learn what it is to be healthy. You can find inner peace and satisfying nightly rest without resorting to drugs. The prescriptions you or those you know have been dependent upon for handling stress and exhaustion are only contributing to the problems you are trying to escape. They are unnatural and unnecessary.

Many sleeping-pill users are having serious problems from an ingredient that is finally being phased out of most such products. However, it can still be found in some medications and you should be aware of the danger. This is bromide, and the problem people are facing is bromide intoxication.

What happens when someone has too much bromide in his or her system? Sometimes hallucinations. Other times a feeling that people are after him or her. Bad breath can be a symptom, and a few people have violent tremors and delusions.

Often the result of bromide poisoning has been hospitalization in the psychiatric ward of a hospital where additional tranquilizers are prescribed. The problem is self-perpetuating, the treatment actually being the sole cause.

Valerie was a commercial artist who had just taken the job of assistant art director for a large advertising agency when she came to see me. "I can't sleep at night, Dr. Green. I've been pushing and pushing to get ahead in my field, forcing my mind to work every moment. When I walk the streets, I'm always studying shapes and colors, thinking of new ways to provide visual impact to a client's product. I lie in bed thinking about the next day's work. Even now I know that I'm going to stay in bed thinking about a presentation I have to make tomorrow to the chief account executive in my new firm. It's my first presentation since I got this job and it's extremely important to me."

Valerie's face looked drained. Her eyes were lined and puffy. She sat stiffly, as though her entire body was filled with tension.

"How have you slept in the past?" I asked her.

"I've tried just about everything. Every night I take my pills. It's a ritual like brushing my teeth. Every morning I wake up feeling hung over, and that's gotten to be a ritual, too.

"Pills just don't work for me. I feel like my doctors have always spent their days reading the medical journals, searching for something new to offer me. I'm probably hooked on them by now for all I know. I just think it's time I tried something different, something which maybe will work."

I put Valerie on my plan and she rebelled immediately. "I can't stop the sleeping pills," she said, beginning to cry. "I've tried. God knows I've tried. I was hoping you would give me some magic cure, something I could swallow with a glass of water and have instant peace. Instead, you are talking vitamins. Vitamins won't stop what's wrong with me.

"You have no idea what it is to try and get off sleeping pills. I take them to sleep. If I don't take them, I don't sleep. Then, when I do take them, I worry that maybe I didn't take enough of them. Sometimes I worry that I might build up a tolerance and accidentally overdose. I know I'm constantly working against myself but I can't seem to help it. All I'm certain of is that your vitamins are not going to do anything for me if my sleeping pills haven't been strong enough."

"I repeat what I just said," I told her. "You've got to withdraw from the sleeping pills through the use of vitamins and the rest of my plan." I explained about the dolomite and the B complex vitamins. I showed her how the niacinamide converts her adrenalin into the inert and harmless adrenochrome. I got her to understand that sleep is a natural part of a healthy body and mind. I showed her that pharmaceuticals can create the very stress she is trying to avoid when she lies down to go to sleep.

Valerie reluctantly agreed to try my plan. She took slightly less sleeping medication that night, just as I have shown you how to do, then began a regimen that included the vitamins necessary to help her. At first she used L-tryptophane. After three somewhat restless nights, Valerie began sleeping soundly. Each week she reduced her sleeping medication by more and more. Finally she was sleeping drug-free. She stopped needing the extra vitamins before going to bed and just let the regular plan handle her stress.

"This is the most amazing program I've ever encountered," said Valerie. "There are no drugs, no magic formulas. It's just good sense. My body was designed to take care of itself and this means getting adequate rest. I was creating my own problems by adding to its burdens with the drugs."

The fallacy with all sleeping compounds and tranquilizers prescribed each year is that you can't fight stress with stress. Valerie was concerned about how her artistic creations would be accepted. Other patients have worried about the house payments, a spouse in the hospital, paying the cost of higher education, keeping a job. Sometimes the pressures we encounter—divorce, a new boss, change in job, or whatever—keep us awake at night. We allow them to dominate our thoughts and then panic as the clock passes from hour to hour through the night. We go to work tired the next day, then worry about not sleeping that night in addition to our concerns about whatever has come to pass during the day.

Eventually we feel desperate for rest. We go to the doctor, complaining that we can't sleep. The doctor typically prescribes a sleeping pill or a tranquilizer. The doctor also knows that the typical patient will go away satisfied with a pill. The prescription seems the ideal answer for everyone.

The fallacy in this procedure is that the pill adds stress because of the way the medication passes through the body. This is eventually translated into increased anxiety, which leads us to take yet more medication. We slowly become addicted to a course of treatment that does nothing but feed on itself. We still have concerns over that divorce, our future in the job, or the spouse in the hospital. Nothing that was troubling us has changed, and we now have an additional difficulty to face.

The sleeping-pill trap can result in another concern as well. This is the problem of depression and the use of various mood-altering compounds meant to help us feel better.

Medical researchers have discovered that when someone has difficulty sleeping, the serotonin level of the blood is lowered from the insomnia. Serotonin helps the passage of nerve impulses. When the serotonin level is down, it is like having a telephone switchboard in which all the calls are being improperly routed. We cannot function effectively and depression follows. However, L-tryptophane actually raises the level of serotonin in the brain. Depression is likewise eliminated or reduced to a level we can easily overcome without medication.

One study in Suffolk, England, by medical researchers A. D. Broadhurst and Dapji Rao took severely depressed patients and randomly divided them into two groups. One group was given a common, widely prescribed antidepressant drug while the second group was given just a quarter ounce of L-tryptophane. At the end of four weeks, the group receiving L-tryptophane had eliminated its depression with no further problems. The people receiving the antidepressant drug, the common way for many doctors to handle such a problem, continued to have difficulties coping. The L-tryptophane could be stopped and the people continued feeling good about themselves, though they did have to watch their diet. The antidepressant medication had to be continued or they tended to drift immediately back into the depressed state.

Sometimes the real problem of insomnia is a suppressed anger. Rhoda's face showed signs of what she claimed was a natural part of getting older. Many of the "natural" marks of aging indicate muscle tension, the exterior sign of interior turmoil. The majority of my clients, Rhoda included, discover that their skin texture and the relaxed muscles in their faces within a month or two of living without pharmaceutical dependency makes them look years younger.

Rhoda told me her story was one of lost love.

> I met David eleven years ago. He was the most beautiful man I had ever seen. He was tall, handsome, intelligent, and totally committed to making me over into something he felt would be far greater than my normal self. I was an undergraduate student in college and he was studying to be a doctor. My hair was drab, my features were plain. I was a nondescript mouse. Yet David saw something special in me. He told me that I could be a model. He told me that if I would change my appearance and the way I walked and talked, I could be extremely successful.
>
> I didn't know if David was serious or not and I really didn't care. I believed him . . . I wanted to believe him. He saw me as a beauty when I saw myself as a young drudge. I let him take me to hair stylists and model agencies and photographers. I did look better than I ever had before and apparently I did have talent. I got my first modeling job and David was thrilled.
>
> Then, slowly, our relationship changed. I realized David was trying to use me. He said he didn't have the money to pay for his next semester of medical school and I asked about his parents because I thought they were paying his way. He told me that he was doing it on his own and that he had become so infatuated with me he had stopped working for a while in order to devote all his attention to making me over into a model. Since I was finally beginning to make big money in my field, he thought I should help him. Like a fool, I decided that it was the least I could do for him.

After that I found I was actually keeping David. I paid for his apartment. I paid for his food. I even bought him expensive designer clothing just because he said that he had always wanted it. I loved him so much I didn't think he was using me. I figured he would get through medical school and we would be married. He would earn money and support us when he could. It was like I was in a dream world and never knew it.

Then I discovered I was pregnant. We had always talked about having children one day and he said he loved the idea of a family. However, when it actually happened, he wasn't very pleased. We were living together and I felt married so I didn't see why we couldn't work things out.

David said no. I had to get an abortion and he made sure it was arranged. I checked into the hospital, had my abortion and then, before I could leave, I received a telegram from him.

A telegram. My God, the nerve of that man! Can you imagine getting a telegram in the hospital the day of your abortion and having it say that the man you loved was getting married to some girl I never heard of? That's what David did. He sent me a telegram saying he was marrying someone else. I don't even know when he had time to date anyone else. I thought it was a hideous, cruel, practical joke.

It wasn't a joke. When I got out of the hospital, David and this girl left for Spain. I couldn't even confront him to find out what had happened between us. It was horrible and there was absolutely nothing I could do to change anything.

I had known things were different between us. The problem had been that I was working night and day handling modeling assignments, while he was studying for exams. Our sex life had diminished but we both knew the intense schedules we were keeping were temporary. We both knew things would change shortly. We both enjoyed just the few moments of touching and being close which sometimes represented all the time we had together. Yet somehow David met another woman and had an affair with her.

Eventually I learned all that happened. David went to Spain, toured Europe with this woman, and ended up marrying in London. He got his MD degree and returned to Manhattan to set up practice. He never tried to call me again.

I had to contact him. I had to try and get some perspective on what had happened between us even though months had passed since all this took place. I called him, told him it was me, and was shocked to hear him react so coldly. He said that I had helped him become a doctor and he had helped me become a model. We had both profited from our relationship and that was what mattered. It was all over. We had paid each other tit for tat. There was nothing more to be said. I should go out and find myself another man because he had a wife now and couldn't be bothered with me.

It was all so cold, so unexpected. I loved David so much. I loved the man I thought him to be and I couldn't handle what I was hearing. It was like he had stabbed me in the heart. The pain in my chest was overwhelming. I cried and cried. My God, I didn't think the tears would end.

Finally I went to see my doctor. I wasn't sleeping except those nights when I cried myself to sleep. He gave me sleeping pills and I've been taking them ever since. It's the only way I can blot out the pain at night. It's the only way I can handle the horrible stress under which I've been living.

But now I see that the sleeping pills are causing as many problems as David. I can't sleep without them, and lately they haven't been working. I feel like I've become old before by time and, in my business, that can destroy you.

Dr. Green, can you help me?

I realized that Rhoda's problems were actually twofold. There was her sleeping pill abuse, of course. But there was something more. From the way she talked about David, it was obvious that Rhoda was not fully in touch with her feelings. She had never faced how she now felt toward David. She had suppressed her true emotions much too long.

I had Rhoda relive her relationship with David. I had her close her eyes and start talking about where they met, where they went on their dates, the good times they shared, and how they had moved in together. Then she reached the part of the story where she had the abortion. I had her face her feelings both when she learned she was pregnant and when she realized David was abandoning her the day she got her abortion.

It was humiliating, Dr. Green. That damned bastard made me feel like the biggest fool in the world. I worshiped that man. Jesus, I let him make me over. I felt that he was the one who had made me a model. I never saw my own hard work. I never saw the hours and hours of training. I never saw all the time I spent making the rounds. I just remembered the little bit of encouragement David had given me and made him like a god in my eyes.

I was such a fool. He had deceived me. He had used me for his own ends, then thrown me away like a disposable. I felt that everything he had ever told me was a lie. We lived together for years and suddenly I felt like I could never believe anything he had ever said to me.

I felt like I had been an ass all my adult life. I wondered if my friends knew the truth. I wondered if the whole damned world was laughing at me. I hated the bastard and I hated myself for ever loving him. Yet I did love him. In many ways he's a fine man. I loved him. I hated him. . . .

But I should hate him. Oh, maybe not hate him, but certainly not respect him. He was rotten and manipulative. I trusted him and he betrayed that trust. I'm a far better person than he is today and I see now that I don't need to keep making him the focal point of my life.

Finally Rhoda stopped crying. Her eyes were red, yet she seemed somehow far more relaxed than when she first stepped into my office. She had finally talked out her feelings, something you will learn later in this book, and now she had begun to find inner peace.

"I feel numb, Dr. Green. I feel as if my anger has really gone away. Yet there is something I still want to say to him."

"Then say it," I told Rhoda. "Pretend he is sitting in that empty chair near you. Tell him whatever it is you are feeling now. Don't hold back. You've got to express yourself."

Rhoda turned to the chair, looking at it as she might if David were truly there. Her face softened as she said "I love you. I don't feel badly about loving you. I love you because you were, in that time and that space, good for me. I outgrew you and you outgrew me. We grew in different directions and I tried to hang on, just as you tried to hang on. Now you are with somebody else. That's all right and I realize that I have to find somebody else. It was just the way things ended that was so bad, so wrong."

Rhoda turned back to me and said "You know, love is a funny thing. There are all sorts of different types of love. There is neurotic love—symbiotic and dominated by sexual drive. I think my love with David was like that. He always satisfied me sexually and somehow I felt secure with him, especially since I expected him to marry me.

"I think he resented my helping him even though he wanted it. I never realized that he could resent me for giving him what I thought he wanted from me. But I also knew that the past is past. That experience is over. I have to live in the present." She looked back at the empty chair and said "Goodbye, David. Goodbye, forever."

When Rhoda left my office, she was serene and joyous. She had finally faced the real cause of her insomnia and talked it out through the technique of visualizing the person involved and saying all those things she needed to say. She was still dependent on sleeping pills, but she knew that the plan would be the solution. The underlying stress, her failed relationship with David, was finally brought out into the open and understood and accepted. The inner turmoil her doctors had never addressed with sleeping pills was finally ended.

Today Rhoda is happily married to a mature man who is both supportive of her and accepting of her support of him. They love and help each other, busy in separate careers, yet close in their relationship and mutual respect. She has not always had perfect nights since she saw me, but she has also never considered the need for a sleeping pill. A little dolomite, some B complex vitamins, and Vitamin C are the natural ways she handles the occasional stress she faces.

Another factor in gaining normal sleep is understanding your body's natural rhythm. Everyone has an inner clock attuned to twenty-four-hour living. Our body temperature changes by a total of approximately two degrees in the course of any given day. It is usually lowest during the time we sleep and reaches a peak in the late afternoon. Regular sleeping hours ensure that we keep our body's clock from giving false signals. Having a fairly set pattern of sleep allows us to adjust so that we become tired at bedtime and alert during the waking hours. This only becomes a problem when someone changes schedules, as when a day worker transfers to nights. However, even this requires only a day or two of adjustment, perhaps helped by the vitamins needed to ensure our rest.

Waking up in the morning is something else. Some people leap from the bed, singing operatic arias, dancing about the room, and mentally calculating mathematical problems that would have stumped Einstein at his best. Other people awaken slowly. They grope about the room, curse the thunder of a piece of dog hair being shed against the carpeted floor, and otherwise travel in a fog for several minutes. Neither is better than the other, and both relate to the body rhythm of the particular individual.

It's important to understand your own needs and plan for them. It helps to sleep in one stretch rather than constantly interrupted periods, because of the REM level mentioned earlier.

According to recent studies of sleep, REM sleep occurs with all manner of internal happenings, including dreams that are seldom remembered the next day. The head and neck muscles are so relaxed that they would be unable to support your head if you were able to sit up. A sudden awakening at this time leaves you with the sensation of being paralyzed, though you are not. Your breathing is rapid, shallow, and uneven in such a circumstance and your heartbeat and blood pressure will fluctuate widely. The brain's temperature rises and hormones related to the adrenal glands are stimulated.

There are actually four states of sleep, as noted earlier, and this cycle of stages repeats itself throughout the night. Usually you reach the REM level for just ten minutes during the first cycle. You will probably hit four to six REM periods in the course of a normal night.

Your sleeping pattern goes from a light sleep to a deeper level. You travel downward to the deepest, most restful level if you are not awakened or not blocked by the chemicals within sleeping pills. This calm and refreshing sleep you can't get with drugs.

Researchers are uncertain about all that happens when you sleep through the deep REM stage. One researcher believes that it is at this deepest level that your brain is able to sort out the events of the day. Facts are stored in your head, problems solved, and priorities of thought sorted. If this theory is accurate, it accounts for one of the reasons sleeping-pill users never awaken fully rested or refreshed. They feel groggy, hung-over, and unable to think clearly. They never achieve the REM level, where the jumble of facts, experiences, and mental stimulations achieved through the day can be placed in a semblance of order.

The diet recommended for getting off tranquilizers has a potent effect on sleep problems as well. For example, inositol is part of the B complex vitamins and is also an antidote to insomnia. Researchers have found that inositol reduces stress and can help lower blood pressure. It is found naturally in wheat germ, whole wheat, oats, corn, barley, oranges, grapefruit, apples, cantaloupe, tomatoes, green peas, carrots, cabbage, spinach, peanuts, yeast, and other foods. Wheat germ is a primary source of inositol, with 6.9 mg. (Beef has just 2.6 mg.)

Inositol is also available as a food supplement. If you are having great difficulty with your sleep, you might try taking as much as 1000 or 2000 mg in the evening as a dietary supplement.

Please keep in mind that the dolomite, L-tryptophane, inositol, and other bedtime vitamin supplements meant to help you sleep are not part of the long-term program for staying off tranquilizers. These vitamins, minerals, and—in the case of L-tryptophane—are meant to help you change your pattern and get through the withdrawal period. Once you rid your body of pharmaceuticals which have just been adding to your stress, you will find that you fall into a natural cycle of sleep. You will be naturally relaxed and only need the dolomite, and so forth, when unusual circumstances arise which would otherwise keep you from sleeping.

Sandor had a slightly different problem from some of my patients. He was an insomniac who seemed unable to sleep at night yet was unable ever truly to be awake during the day. He was constantly drowsy on the job, yet his mind seemed to race once he lay down in bed. He would get up and watch late-night television for a while, go back to bed, get up to read a book, go back to bed, get up to go to the bathroom, and on and on in a vicious cycle. He was divorced because his wife said his constant roaming kept her awake, and he agreed he was difficult to live with. He had taken everything from a good stiff shot of whiskey before bedtime to the sleeping pill Dalmane. None worked, yet he became addicted to the pills, which he took night after night, hoping that one evening a miracle would take place and he would finally get adequate rest. He didn't. Sandor had leg cramps at night which added to his sleep problems. This was cured with 500 milligrams of magnesium at night. The addition of magnesium induced restfulness.

Questioning Sandor about his background, I learned that doctors he had seen in the recent past had ruled out any medical problems as being the cause of his drowsiness accompanied by insomnia. Then I asked about his eating habits. I found his meals were primarily highly processed foods with high sugar content. He was deficient in the B complex vitamins, especially pantothenic acid.

Sleep researchers have learned that pantothenic acid missing from the body can cause the very symptom Sandor had been experiencing for months. He tried just adding 1000 mg of pantothenic acid to his diet in the morning and a second 1000-mg tablet in the afternoon. The first night he began sleeping better and found that the following day he was more alert.

He found that when he added 200 mg magnesium to his diet, he was no longer restless. He also added 400 mg calcium, because it helps the body absorb the magnesium faster and more thoroughly. A lack of calcium actually results in the body's blocking most of the magnesium it needs, in effect doubling the problem.

Many of my clients come to me dispirited and hopeless. Their belief in themselves has been given up to chemicals; they are out of touch with their own possibilities. Their minds and bodies are clouded. Once their senses and perceptions return, they feel renewal and hope. Their belief in their ability to make decisions and direct their life returns. As they get stronger and think more clearly, they have no fear of lapsing back into the buffered world of artificial fixes. They have the zest of a new life. They can sleep without sleeping pills.

The power is within you to start a new life without sleeping pills. Once you know you have the power, you must know how to turn it on.

7

Meditation
from Alpha to Theta

Getting a good night's sleep is an essential part of leading a tranquilizor froo oxiotonoo. But ao you loarn to doal with stress naturally, it is important that you also learn to relax during the day. Relaxing results in lowered pulse rate, slower breathing, and other physiological changes that release the body from tension and make it easier for you to face even the worst upsets your day can bring.

The relaxation method you will probably find easiest to incorporate into your normal day is a form of meditation—fractional relaxation. You can do this exercise without any special preparations.

Meditation can be done by anyone. It is a method for using your own mind to help you relax. There is nothing magical about it. A few minutes before going to work, during a coffee break, in the evening, just before going to bed, is all it takes.

We all have inner protection against stress overload. Initially the stress, whether it is a family argument, trying to maneuver on a crowded freeway, or even a mugger lurking in the shadows, creates a "fight-or-flight" response. Our adrenalin flows and we are prepared to take a physical stand or to flee the danger with all due speed.

Our ancestors needed the fight-or-flight response because in their surroundings they were constantly faced with life-or-death situations such as finding protection from giant animals or the wild elements.

Over the millennia we have learned to use reason instead of physicality, with at least some degree of success. But some of our biochemical responses dating from earlier times remain potent forces. Our adrenalin, for example, still flows with the fight-or-flight syndrome.

To avoid being so powerfully affected by our harsh body chemistry, sometimes we have to slow down our reactions. Although niacinamide converts the adrenalin to adreno-chrome, it does not handle the emotional anxiety. For this you need the technique of meditation.

Meditation is actually very simple. There are four prerequisites. The first is that you find a quiet environment. This does not mean a soundproof room or high mountaintop. It just means any location where you will not keep focusing on the sounds all around you. One of my patients was a reporter who worked in the busy city room of a metropolitan newspaper. He had learned to tune out the sounds of typing and frenzied activity in order to meet his deadlines. He could close his eyes and have all the quiet he needed, right there at his desk, in the large, open room.

Other patients have used different techniques. One meditated in the rest room. Another went into the closetlike room where office supplies were kept. Yet another went to a different part of the office complex that was equally noisy, but where he knew no one would try to reach him.

The second step is to find a mental device to focus on to channel your thinking away from the cares of the day. Some groups speak of a *mantra* and utilize elaborate rituals. A mantra is only a word repeated to oneself in order to concentrate attention. It is only one way of getting yourself focused.

The third step is adopt a passive attitude. In effect you are saying that for the next five to ten minutes you are going to relax and let all your tensions go. You are not going to let your mind be interrupted by the cares of the world.

Finally, you need to take a comfortable position. You can sit on your desk, the floor, a couch, lie down, or do anything else you find comfortable.

Once you are comfortable, recognize that for the first five to ten minutes you are going to concentrate on nothing. Nothing at all. Any thoughts that come to mind will be allowed to drift through your head like clouds floating through the sky on a windy day. Do not attempt to focus on them. Do not attempt to make note of what you must do in the next few minutes. Instead, let distracting thoughts pass through your mind and continue your efforts to relax.

Some people feel they can make the transition to a state of full relaxation faster if they first concentrate on their breathing. They begin breathing slowly, evenly, through their nostrils. They concentrate on this breathing, inhaling, exhaling, inhaling, exhaling, letting their minds stay as clear as possible. Thoughts of the afternoon meeting, the evening date, the constantly ringing telephone are all allowed to pass without getting into them. The cares and ideas of the day will be waiting for "you when you are relaxed. For the moment, your concern is with temporarily finding inner peace so you can work calmly and effectively the rest of the day.

Don't worry about how well you are relaxing. Each time you try this exercise you will relax faster and more completely. The important point is to start without setting any arbitrary standards for your success.

After you have begun to drift into the pattern of rhythmical breathing, you will begin to relax your body. This is done by concentrating on each part of your body, visualizing it, and telling it to relax.

Start by thinking of your toes. Mentally sense your toes relaxing. All the stiffness and tension is being drained from them. They are relaxing more and more.

Now concentrate on the soles of your feet, the balls of your feet, your ankles, your lower legs, your knees, and on and on. Concentrate on one section of your body at a time, mentally picturing it relaxing. Work your way from your toes through the top of your head. You can take each part a few seconds or a few minutes at a time, depending upon how much time you have to spend. You might want to use a period in the early morning or evening to relax completely for twenty to thirty minutes. This will probably not be possible in the office, where far less time can be utilized.

There should be no distractions during the time you are relaxing, if this is possible. Try to avoid using an alarm clock to signal when to stop. If this is necessary at first because of where you follow the relaxation technique, try to set aside some time each week when you can meditate for twenty minutes.

What happens with this meditative device? There are several different brain waves everyone is capable of experiencing, depending upon the circumstances.

First is the delta wave. Known as the unconscious wave because it is often experienced by people who are deeply sleeping.

The beta wave is probably the brain wave you are experiencing at this very moment. It is commonly called the rational wave because it exists when you are reading, figuring numbers, or engaged in activities that call upon your senses. You also experience the beta wave when eating.

It is the alpha wave that is the key to meditation. The alpha wave is the wave of creativity and growth. In other cultures it is called *satori* or *samadhi* or the yoga state of contemplation.

The theta wave is even higher than the alpha wave but is not of real concern so far as getting off tranquilizers is concerned. It is the state in which we can experience telepathy, clairvoyance, ESP, phenomena we call paranormal.

The meditative exercise involving relaxation of different parts of your body leads to the alpha brain wave. Most of my patients find that after they have practiced a few minutes of meditation a day to quiet their minds and bodies they can achieve instant alpha just by pausing in what they are doing and concentrating on their breathing. They make their minds silent. Often they will do this during a time of intense stress, closing their eyes for a moment, clearing their minds of thoughts and concentrating on slow breathing through their nose. For just a couple of seconds they will inhale deeply, exhale slowly, inhale deeply, and exhale slowly. No one realizes they are doing anything out of the ordinary, but when they stop they have the serenity they need to handle the crisis.

Jennifer's case is typical of what can happen when you raise your brain waves to relax. She worked in a small financial consulting firm. The business had started with an individual and grew over three years. The staff enlarged every few months, each new person usually starting at the bottom. Jennifer began as secretary, even though she had an advanced degree in the field with which the firm was involved. She proved her value to the company and gradually moved higher. She gained her own accounts and knew that, if she kept progressing at the same rate, she would be at the top.

Jennifer was my client when she first started with the financial consulting firm. She was dependent on tranquilizers and sleeping pills, which had been first prescribed by the student health center at the Midwestern university from which she received her master's degree. She was told her problems were the result of "nerves" and she accepted this idea because her family had a history of hypertension and heart disease.

The pill use had become prescription abuse and Jennifer knew she couldn't continue taking a tranquilizer to handle the stress of her job and a sleeping pill to put her to sleep at night. What she didn't know until she started to play was that her family's "nervous problems" were probably related to their high-sugar, high-starch diet. Jennifer went to a medical doctor for the Seale Harris glucose tolerance test and discovered that she was hypoglycemic. She quickly corrected this through her diet.

Jennifer found that the meditation technique helped her through the day. She would use it for ten minutes in the morning, after walking. She repeated this technique before facing rush-hour traffic, and also used it during the day if pressure became overwhelming.

Then one day Jennifer discovered just how much control a person can have over his or her life when alpha is used. It was the day Jennifer was fired and came to see me immediately afterward.

I never thought I could lose my job with the firm. I had moved up so quickly that I was certain I was doing well. They had just given me my own accounts to handle and, though I had very few, I was beginning to make things grow. I knew that within a few months I would have generated enough new business to have more than a full load.

Then everything went wrong. My boss came over to my desk and didn't even have the nerve to look at me. His eyes were staring at the papers as he mumbled that the company was going to have to let me go. He didn't say why or what I had done wrong.

My first reaction was one of horror. I wanted to scream at him. I wanted to know what I had done that was so terrible that all of a sudden I'd get fired after being moved up so quickly. I was being given thirty days' notice, as though that would pay for all the work and love that had gone into the job.

I knew a lot of the people in the office took Valium and that was my next reaction. I had constantly downed those "blues" before I came to see you and now I wanted to run back to them. They were familiar friends I knew I could use to escape. I wanted to take one or two and drift off into a different world where I didn't have to think.

But that would have been running from myself, Dr. Green. You've taught me that I can't deal with stress by running to a pill because the problem is still there when I get back. Yet I didn't feel as though I could face the crisis I was in either. I didn't know what to say or do.

Then I remembered what you said about the meditation. I closed my eyes and forced my mind to be empty. I took a couple of slow breaths through my nose and focused on the nothingness. Then I opened my eyes and spoke more calmly than I ever thought possible under the circumstances.

I told my boss that I understood what he was saying. I said that I felt his decision was not a good one because I was one of the best employees he had. I said that I thought we should talk over the situation so I could understand exactly why the company wanted me to leave.

We went into his office and he finally admitted that my work was perfect. The problem was with the firm's cash flow. Every account executive had to be earning money in excess of salary and overhead or the company was in trouble. Because I was the newest person in that position, it would be at least a few weeks before I could reach that level. In the meantime, they had to let me go even though they knew that eventually I would probably be the office's biggest producer.

Once I knew the situation I was able to offer a compromise. I agreed to take a temporary cut in pay for the next ninety days, my actual pay being deferred until they were through the cash-flow crisis. Instead of running away to a tranquilizer, I used your meditation technique to achieve instant alpha. That gave me the calm to handle the crisis constructively. Instead of being fired, I still have a job and the chance for the future I've always wanted. I didn't really meditate but I did totally calm myself. I gained a control I know would have been impossible otherwise.

Another way to achieve instant alpha in an emergency situation is through what is known as nostril breathing. This is just another way of focusing your mind and becoming totally relaxed without drugs. You cover one nostril and breathe in through the open side. Then you cover the opposite nostril and exhale through the side you had previously closed. You repeat this procedure a few times and you will find yourself relaxing. Several of my patients do this in situations such as freeway traffic jams where it is impossible for them to get away or even to close their eyes as an aid to relaxing. Naturally they have all learned to relax first through the approach of gradually relaxing each part of their bodies, but this is accomplished very quickly.

Meditation can be used to bring about a change in your life

and emotional attitudes. Once you are in the alpha state, your mind is more receptive to new concepts, positive action, and creativity.

Each of us is like a computer programmer, with the human mind being the computer. We get back only that information which is fed into our computer. If that information is negative, our thoughts and actions can work against us. When the information is positive, our thoughts and actions work to our advantage.

Most people who become addicted to tranquilizers, sleeping pills, and antidepressants have developed negative attitudes. They are plagued with *nots*. "I am *not* going to get that raise." "My wife, husband, lover *won't* love me anymore." "I am doomed to be drug dependent the rest of my life." I can't. I won't. It's impossible—On and on and on, into total despondency.

It is hard to change that negative thinking pattern without alpha because it is in alpha that we reach the unconscious where the negative computer programming exists. It is fine to say "Today I am going to go after that promotion, tell my lover that he isn't satisfying my needs, and start feeling better about myself." However, if you have not changed your inner computer program, your subconscious mind is busy saying, "You'll make a fool of yourself asking for a raise, your lover will still reject you, and why should you like yourself when you aren't worth anything?"

The alpha state reaches your "computer program center" and restructures it toward a positive thought direction by helping you see the big picture and regain your perspective. We can become the best within us through the slight expansion of the meditative technique we are already using to find peace without tranquilizers.

For example, suppose you have just taken a few minutes to reach the alpha state. Perhaps it is early morning, late at night, or on the weekend. You are not pressured by your job, family, or other pressures. You feel you can spare the time needed to grow beyond your negative programming. You decide to take a few extra minutes to discover a new internal

strength which can change your life for the better. This is
what you do:

First, I want you to experience the limitless aspect of your
mind. Most of us think of our physical bodies as the
boundaries of our existence. In reality, the mind can take you
into dimensions you have never thought possible, freeing
you from all physical constraints without using drugs or any
other potentially destructive device.

Start by using the fractional relaxation technique already
described, then begin to do what I call visualization. This is a
simple exercise meant to expand your awareness of yourself
in relation to the world around you.

Once you are fully relaxed, visualize the four corners of
the room. Try to get a mental picture of the room, though you
need not worry about the details. Concentrate on the space
all around you rather than trying to picture plants, wall
hangings, bookshelves, or anything else.

Now become that space. Pull it into you so that you feel as
though you are filling the vastness. Don't allow your mind to
dwell on any subject. Let your thoughts be silent. Experience
the expanse of the room and notice how relaxed you become.
You are floating free from anxiety and stress. You are
separate from your anxieties, totally relaxed.

Now slowly expand your consciousness. Visualize the fact
that you are part of the planet earth. You are part of the giant
mass of land and sea traveling through space. Experience
this great expanse, far more vast than just the room in which
you are relaxing, and know that you are a part of it. Mentally
visualize yourself becoming one with the planet.

Some of my patients have trouble creating visual imagery
in this manner. For them, I suggest just thinking about the
concepts. It is better to visualize while in alpha, to actually
try to see the land and water, the vast continents and billions
of people, but visualization is not essential. Just thinking
about this concept can have powerful effects for change as
well.

Next take the concept still further. Visualize yourself as
part of the galaxy. Visualize the vast reaches of space within
our solar system, the planets, the moons, the darkness and

the light. Make yourself a part of the solar system. Feel it all around you. Mentally become one with it, letting yourself expand to reach its vast immensity.

Finally, imagine yourself as part of the universe. Visualize yourself as infinite, encompassing all the space, the planets, the galaxies, and the endlessness all around us. You will be floating free, at peace, greater than you have ever been despite the fact that your physical body has never left the room in which you first began the fractional relaxation exercise.

How wonderful it is to be a part of the endlessly pulsating cosmos! Can you feel the universal life source all around? Can you feel the universal mind, which is now part of your mind? Let the energy of this experience flow into your entire being. You are coming to peace with the strength of life forces infinitely greater than your body, and you are growing with the experience.

After several days of trying this exercise to take you beyond the alpha state normally achieved in fractional relaxation, you may want some variety. One possibility was developed by Dr. Roberto Assaglio, founder of psychosynthesis, and expounded in the books *Act of Will* and *Psychosynthesis*. His visualization exercises are geared to helping each of us reach the higher self.

The higher self is the part of the mind which has all the deepest answers. You may not have liked yourself in the past. You may have tried tranquilizers because you did not feel that you had the inner strength to solve life's problems. All of us have an inner power that can be tapped for every answer we might ever need. Many people do not recognize the existence of this power waiting to help them, so they do not know to look inside themselves for the answers.

Once you have completed the fractional relaxation, visualize a large meadow at the foot of a mountain. It is a perfect day, the sun is warming your body, calming you with its gentle heat. The meadow has a gentle breeze and you are at peace.

You glance up the mountain and see a sloping path rising

to the temple of silence. You realize that the path will be easy to travel, and though your journey will take you high into the mountain, you know that it will not be too strenuous. You feel you must reach the temple of silence and that any exertion, no matter how strenuous, is worth the effort. However, as you visualize yourself climbing the mountain, feeling the change in elevation and the mild stress of walking up the path, you are pleased to find yourself going toward the temple of silence. You know it is where you will find some answers and the exertion of the trip is not so great as you first anticipated.

Now you are reaching the top of the path and you see the clearing in which the temple of silence is located. You pause for a moment, taking in the beauty of the temple and feeling the tremendous peace which radiates from the temple.

You enter the clearing and your body becomes filled with silence. Everything is quiet and relaxed. You know you have made the right decision in climbing the mountain and now you are experiencing a peace that is more calming than anything you have over known.

Step into the temple. Notice the light beam radiating down through the center of the temple. It is the energy of silence and that light permeates your body, granting you a serenity you never thought possible. Your mind is still, yet alert to each new experience that might befall you. You bask in the warmth of the light, your feelings calmed, your mind silent.

After a few moments you notice a staircase leading to the roof of the temple. You climb it, winding through the light to the top where you can see the radiant sun beaming down all around you.

In the middle of the sun is an infinitely wise being. You study its face and see that it is gentle, filled with love just for you. What you are encountering is your inner self—the part of you to which you can turn for answers to every question you might have about yourself.

What troubles you? What questions do you have? What are your cares for this day and in the immediate future for which you feel the need for answers? Consult this part of your inner essence. Tell it everything, speaking aloud or silently to yourself, whichever is comfortable. It is part of you, so it will hear your thoughts, your personal questions, and entreaties.

Tell the "being" what is bothering you. Discuss the choices you have to make in the near future and ask for advice. Whatever information you seek will be provided. Trust this intuition. You know more than you think you know.

Another approach to theta involves positive visualization. You meditate through the fractional relaxation technique, then expand your awareness of the universe as described. Now create a positive thought and hold it directly in front of you. Next visualize this same positive thought on each side, behind you, above and below you. Each time you do this, hold it for a few seconds, then pull it in so that you become a part of it.

What is a positive thought? It can be anything that is right for you. For example, Norman, one of my clients, was concerned about his future in the bank where he worked as a teller. His assistant manager intimidated him. He feared the man and made mistakes whenever the assistant manager supervised his work. At other times he did quite well.

I had Norman get into a theta state through the techniques I have shown you. Then he visualized the positive thought of seeing himself shaking hands with his assistant manager. Norman was standing by the teller's window and the assistant manager was smiling happily at him.

The visualization of the positive thought of his assistant manager being happy with him made Norman more self-confident. He repeated this technique twice a day for almost two weeks before putting it to the test. Then, on a rather hectic Thursday, Norman again had to deal with his assistant manager's supervision of his work.

> I can't tell you how happy I am, Dr. Green. I didn't make one mistake on Thursday [said Norman when he came to see me the following Monday]. I discovered that I really wasn't frightened of my boss. I saw him in an entirely different light. I was relaxed, self-confident, and I realize that for the first time I didn't see him as a threat.

It didn't go just like my positive visualization. I reached a point towards the end of the day when I felt as though he might shake my hand, smile at me and promote me to head teller or something. But that didn't happen.

What did happen is that he seemed to see me in a different way. Maybe my past tension was sending out negative vibrations or something. I didn't really believe that, of course, but something like that probably was happening. In any case, he told me he liked my work and my attitude. He said that management had its eye on me and he felt I had a good future with the bank.

Then, on Friday, he smiled at me when I walked in the door. He's never smiled at me before. It was as though he was glad that I worked in his office and that made me feel really good. He was friendly all day today, too. I tell you, Dr. Green, it's like everything's changed because I changed myself. My attitude is different from what it was and I owe it all to the positive visualization I've been doing each day.

There are other thoughts you can hold during this period, depending upon your needs. For example, Wilma was probably in the worst condition of anyone I'd ever seen—she was addicted to not one but several tranquilizers. "I've been on the drugs since they were first invented and sometimes I think I was the person they experimented with so they wouldn't hurt the rats."

Meditation can have powerful effects with neurological dysfunction. Wilma, a handsome brunette school teacher, spoke with odd facial movements. The sad part of Wilma's experience was that her problems over the years were minor. The way in which her doctors handled them caused complications that had caused tardive dyskinesia.

It started with the death of my parents. I was very young when they were killed in a plane crash. Their bodies were badly burned and their faces had to be recreated by the mortician. It was like seeing plastic people when I went to the funeral home with my aunt. She insisted that I kiss them goodbye, but it wasn't my parents I was kissing. I didn't know who those plastic strangers were. It was like going to the wax museum and having someone insist that two figures had once been flesh and blood. It was the most frightening experience I think any child could be put through and I became hysterical. That's when I started with the tranquilizers.

Dr. Green, you can't believe what happened after that. My aunt meant well but she kept taking me to this idiot doctor who decided that if the tranquilizer worked once, it would work again. I'd have trouble with schoolwork, fight with a boyfriend, or have any other upsetting experience and this bastard would order a tranquilizer. He and my aunt seemed to think that I never got over the trauma of my parents' funeral, yet I had. I was a perfectly normal girl growing up, other than that one nightmare. Sure, I got angry one minute and depressed the next, just like every other adolescent. But instead of letting things work themselves out, they got out the tranquilizers. I was some sort of sick object for pity in their eyes, and giving me a pill was a lot easier than talking to me to find out what was really happening.

By the time I got to college, I used tranquilizers as a crutch for everything. I took them when I was nervous about sorority rush and my first date with a campus jock. I took them if my menstrual flow was hurting or if I worried that it was late. I took them after a big exam, telling myself I was so hyper from the intensity of the work that only a tranquilizer would calm me down. I gave up my soul for those damned drugs.

Wilma was in my office because she had come to grips with herself and her problem. She knew what was wrong and was determined to lead a tranquilizer-free existence even though she thought it was too late to escape the damage created by the drugs.

I taught Wilma about getting into the theta state while she was withdrawing. The vitamins, diet changes, and additional exercise were not enough. There were days when the pressures mounted and she felt as though she absolutely had to have a tranquilizer. She did not take one. Her craving was addressed by the choline and the niacinamide. She still wanted something more.

"I know I'm looking for the magic pill to happiness," said Wilma. "And God knows I should be the first person to say there's no such thing. The drug companies might imply that 'blues' or 'yellows' or 'whites' can unlock the Garden of Eden, but all they do is send you to the pits of Hell. Yet I still want something that will make all this a little easier. Is that silly of me?"

"Of course not, Wilma. All your life you have been taught to run away to have peace. You ran away to the tranquilizers and now that you are getting off the drugs, running away is still uppermost in your mind. What you don't realize is that you can run away in a positive manner."

I explained about the ways to enter theta that I have shown you. However, I suggested to Wilma that she create the ultimate tranquilizing experience in her mind. "Once you have done this fractional relaxation and become one with the universe, visualize the most serene experience you can have. Mentally transport yourself to an island paradise if you like. Have yourself lying in a hammock, native men waving palm fronds to keep you cool. Or go to a lake, on top of a high mountain, or any other mental image that makes you feel serene. Feel the way the sun bakes your body. There are no telephones. Whatever could bother you is being handled by someone else. You will feel relaxed, tranquil, at peace within yourself."

Wilma tried the theta technique, though for her serenity was mentally being on a horse and riding rapidly across the Kansas farm country where she was raised by her parents. She made this image be her serenity when she did her exercises for meditation.

The nicest part about Wilma's story is that her successful withdrawal went beyond what either of us expected. When she understood what had occurred when she took vitamins, she decided to increase choline. She thought that there might be a chance to restore her nerve so she could have a normal appearance.

It took weeks for Wilma to reach the condition she desired. With the choline, Vitamin B_6, an increase in Vitamin C, and stepped-up intake of niacinamide, Wilma found that the involuntary facial movements stopped.

The use of imagery is very potent when you are in theta. Wilma used it to completely relax herself. Norman used it to create a program for positive growth in business. Some of my patients use the imagery of joy. Others think about hard work paying off when they are in a job that requires seemingly endless turmoil they do not want to face without some immediate reward. You can imagine yourself getting money, getting love, having a positive relationship with a man or woman who is currently somewhat distant. It all works no matter how you do it.

What causes this type of mind imagery to work during theta? I do not know. Some people say it is the power of positive thinking, a proper mental attitude, a positive direction. Others say that the mind expands and we are witnessing the great force within which normally is controlled by lowered brain waves. Whatever the real answer, the important point is that visualizing success, happiness, and similar concepts of a personal nature during fractional relaxation does result in change. You become stronger, healthier, more relaxed for it all and this makes the few minutes a day with a silent mind well worth the effort.

Occasionally I have a patient who is embarrassed about meditation because he or she falls asleep while relaxing. You may fall asleep while trying to meditate the first few times. If you do, try the meditation again and again. Eventually you will be able to both meditate and sleep without having the two become intertwined. Remember that sleep and meditation serve two quite different, equally essential purposes. Each in its own way puts you in touch with your unconscious and higher self and lets you see beyond the tensions and difficulties of the day.

8

The Healing Power
of Talking Things Out

One of the best-kept secrets of the psychiatric field is the healing power of simply talking. Every therapist worthy of his or her couch knows that when a troubled individual actually verbalizes a problem, that patient often "self-heals." The patient sees reality for what it is and grasps the right way to view the situation for healthy emotional growth. This doesn't happen all the time, of course. Many patients definitely need the guidance of a professional counselor to go deeper into the unconscious. But for many—perhaps the majority—of troubled individuals, the simple act of talking things out can work miracles.

You will not want to talk out your troubles alone. I always have my patients work with an understanding, accepting friend, lover, spouse, or similar individual. What they quickly realize is that there is almost magical quality to speech. When you verbalize something, both saying the words and hearing yourself talk, you are able to clarify your understanding of yourself. Problems that seemed over- whelming when you thought about them suddenly are clarified as you put them into words. It is best to use someone you know, and who you feel can give you a balanced and objective hearing.

Stopping tranquilizers and controlling your craving for them through the use of vitamins and nutrition is only a partial solution. The reason you took tranquilizers or sleeping pills in the first place was because you had problems, often deep problems, with which you must come to grips. You need to understand yourself so that you can eliminate the underlying causes. We all have troubles that we can banish only by facing up to them, admitting they exist, and then taking a course of action.

Ideally, we should all have sympathetic listeners who take the role of therapists in our lives. Only the more deeply obscured problems are likely to need the expertise of a trained professional. For most of us most of the time, simply ventilating feelings with a friend in moments of close sharing has enormous therapeutic value.

The need for talking out problems is as old as mankind. Early man often found that in addition to the role of foraging for food, protecting hearth and home, and making clothing, someone was needed to take the role of professional listener. In fact, it is often joked that psychotherapists are practitioners of the world's second oldest profession.

Among the earliest therapists were people called *shamans* who were originally from Siberia. The Tungusian tribe had shamans whose job it was to listen to the problems of others, helping them gain an understanding of themselves. The concept was so successful that other countries also developed it. In Tibet, such people were known as *illubi*. In African tribes, the term *witch doctor* was applied, though this was not meant in the negative way we sometimes take it.

All the cultures where the earliest therapists practiced followed a type of health care known as ayuvedic medicine, a concept which treats the whole person. Someone who is sick is not assumed to just have a physical problem even though that is where the symptoms seem to be revealed. The ayuvedic therapists will also look at the individual's mental state, lifestyle, family relationships, diet, and total body as well as the symptoms of an illness.

The ayuvedic concept may be one of the oldest but it is also one of the best. With all our scientific achievements and the magic pills developed for instant cures, we are returning to the whole-person concept of good health. We are discovering that the total individual must be treated, and that is why the concept of talking-it-out is a part of this book.

A separation of medicine from other forms of health care came gradually over the years. Priests in Europe became the first psychotherapists of more modern times. Tragically, our treatment of the troubled has become compartmentalized. One person treats the body (the medical doctor), another the mind (the therapist), still another might consider only the lifestyle or spirit (the minister). There is no crossing over of effort to insure that the whole person is working on all levels. That is why so many people have become dependent on the magic pills called tranquilizers, sleeping pills, and antidepressants. A medical doctor may not want to take the time to try to understand a patient enough to help him or her change life for the better. It is professionally sanctioned to treat the symptom alone. A psychiatrist may not want to consider the effects of nutrition on a patient, seeing only the psychological abnormalities, and the minister may believe problems result from a lack of spiritual faith.

Talking-it-out exposes negative and positive thoughts—a crucial part of my program. Everyone has different attitudes toward the varied experiences we all face. Some can help us grow as individuals, moving us forward with joy and zest. Other attitudes are negative, pulling us backward with a heavy heart. With a different mental attitude, we could move forward, accomplishing more than we ever thought possible, freeing ourselves, not resigning ourselves to despair, senility, and other preventable curable situations.

Very small children often reveal the therapeutic value of talking out problems. They instinctively do what so many adults wrongly try to avoid. They are highly verbal and willing to express anything that troubles them at the moment it happens. Have you ever noticed how upsets children experience are often forgotten minutes later, after they have cried and talked out their feelings? They do not hold in their difficulties, letting their emotions build until they are physically ill, as we do. They also do not seek a magic pill to transport them away from stress, which will always remain. Instead, they face the problem, deal with it, and are freed to move forward in their lives.

Ramsey's story exemplifies how effective verbalizing feelings can be, particularly if they have been repressed for a long time. Ramsey was an important British politician who came to see me during the time in my life when my practice was based in London. His problem was typical of numerous others I have heard in the other countries where I have spoken and practiced.

Ramsey was a man troubled by migraine headaches. He was wealthy, friendly with the rich and famous, and otherwise a man to be envied. His voice reflected the training of the best British schools. He was also a heavy user of tranquilizers and sleeping tablets even though they never addressed the bane of his life, chronic migraine headaches.

Everything went according to my plan. Ramsey freed himself from tranquilizers and sleeping pills. He looked better, felt better, but yet couldn't stop the migraines.

"I think I would feel fine about everything if I could just eliminate these headaches," said Ramsey. "I've had them so long, they're almost a part of me. Yet it seems like a cancerous part that should be surgically removed."

When people have a problem they cannot understand, the origin goes back to an earlier trauma that is often connected to an earlier trauma, like a string of pearls. Ramsey had undergone extensive medical testing that ruled out all organic origins from a pinched nerve to a tumor. The symptoms were real and I felt safe in assuming that they were obvious symptoms of an underlying, unresolved stress factor.

"When did you first have these headaches, Ramsey?" I asked. "Think back as far as necessary, even into childhood Try to remember the very first time you had a migraine."

Looking back to one's past is a proper first step in talking out a problem. Consider when you first had whatever problem is on your mind. This might be a migraine headache, a cold you cannot shake, a feeling of depression which doesn't seem to relate to any recent experience, or any other physical or emotional problem. The problem can cross over between the physical and the emotional—this is common with asthma or arthritis. These illnesses are stress-related and emotions can trigger attacks.

In the case of Ramsey, the first migraine he remembered was when he went to an exclusive British private school. "That's funny, now that I think about it. The school was the best in England and my parents were thrilled that I attended. Yet I'm fairly certain that's when these headaches started."

"What about just before you went to the school? Where were you then? What was happening to you?"

"I was at a different private school. God, it was the most wonderful place. I still think about it. Even to this day, I don't think any place I ever attended was as nice."

"Why did you make the switch?" I asked.

"My father wanted it. He was very socially conscious and felt that the school to which he sent me was the only one proper for a young gentleman. I wanted to stay where I was, but he thought the switch was best for me. My father told me everything would work out for the best. He said that I would finish the term in one school, then transfer to the other."

As Ramsey spoke, his entire body changed. He was like a small boy again. He was on the verge of tears. Even that day, many years after he had left all schooling, the incident related to what was the equivalent in time of the American elementary school years was extremely traumatic. I had the feeling that Ramsey did not realize just how deeply he felt about all this. I suspected that he had been so concerned with pleasing his father over the years that he refused to face the depth of his disappointment.

The power of verbalizing your problems is that it brings to the surface material that has been suppressed. Details about your past experiences may astonish you once you verbalize them. It is only through talking out these feelings that you come to full understanding.

"I went to the school my father wanted and I hated it. I didn't know anybody there and the interests of the other boys weren't my interests. I was deprived of the pleasures that the other school offered me. I had been learning to ride horseback at the first school and this new one didn't have horses. I longed for the animals and the pleasure of riding across the meadows."

"What did you think was the relationship between the migraines and the new school?"

"There was no relationship. They were both country schools for boys. The new school didn't have horses but the grounds were about the same otherwise. The only real difference was the fact that I hated the place. It was a fine, healthy place to be. It was the only place a young English gentleman should have studied. My father always said that; looking back on it, I can understand his viewpoint."

"But you said that was when the migraines started. You got sick despite the fine country air."

"That's true. I never had the migraines before."

"You never had the migraines before what?"

"Before I went to the school. . . . I never had the migraines before I went to the school. I never had them before the school. . . . You know, there must be a connection."

"My God, I never made the connection before. First I got the migraines and then I got the asthma. It was all after I started there. I remember it vividly now. I never looked back before. I always griped about the pain. I suffered and took my pills and never thought about when it all started. It never seemed to matter, yet now I think it does."

"Why do you think that?" I asked.

The illnesses have always kept me from achieving my full potential. I've been considering running for much higher office than I hold but I've always felt that the asthma makes me too great a risk. I often start wheezing when trying to address large groups, and that is an essential skill for the politician. My father has been disappointed in me, but very understanding.

I'm beginning to think that the illness was not really what I felt it was. I think I've been using my poor health as an excuse to punish my father. Except that it doesn't punish him. It only hurts me. I'm holding myself back. I'm doing all the suffering, and for what? For pain that has been out of my life for more than thirty years.

I'm shocked at myself. I don't need a crutch. I need me. You've taken me off my pills and now I think that by talking out my problems, I'm going to be able to take myself off the illnesses I've been using as an excuse for everything that's been a problem. I don't want my father to feel guilty or suffer through my pain. He meant well even though I think he was wrong to do what he did.

Ramsey left my office with new understanding of himself, understanding that came from talking out the repressed feelings that caused him suffering for twenty years.

Since that day, Ramsey has had neither migraines nor asthma. His health is excellent and he is living free of prescriptions. He has also recognized that he does enjoy his political work and that he has a higher destiny than his position at the time he saw me. At this writing he has begun to achieve important political positions and there is talk that in another few years he might be considered a candidate for prime minister. His asthma was gone.

I am not suggesting that by talking out your problems during and after the time you get off tranquilizers you can make all of life's problems vanish. What you *will* do is become more in harmony with yourself. You will come to understand your fears and negative thoughts and see alternate ways to view what you are experiencing.

Another of my patients, William, wanted desperately to be an established concert musician but had never achieved his dream. He did not seem particularly concerned about all this, though, because when he arrived at my office, it was with a smile on his face and a gleam in his eye. I was curious to hear his story.

"My troubles really don't belong here, I suppose. I have moments when I get so dizzy and weak that I have to lie down. It's affecting my life. The doctors have checked me for high blood pressure, low blood sugar, and everything else. None of the normal causes are there and a friend of mine suggested I try you. You helped her get off Valium and your methods seemed to give her a richer life. She said that you're good with illness when there's no physical cause which can be found by the medical doctor, such as in my case. I just hope you don't think there is no hope for me."

"Once you rule out the organic causes of illness, you usually are left to face the possibility of psychosomatic illness," I explained.

"Are you saying it's all in my head, Doc? Are you saying that I belong in some sort of looney farm?"

"Of course not, I suspect that if we look back into your past and you tell me about when the problem first started, you may find that you were experiencing an emotional situation to which you reacted physically. I suspect that when you talk about this situation, everything will become clear and you can begin to stop the problem."

"Then you want me to tell you about the first time I started to feel dizzy a lot?"

"Yes."

"That goes back a few years. Shortly after I got married. It was a big change in lifestyle for me and I remember the dizziness happening around that time."

"How is your marriage?"

"As good as anybody's."

"What does that mean?"

"Well, at the beginning, the sex was fine. However, after a while I found that it was more fun masturbating." He laughed but I could tell he was really troubled.

"Sex isn't why I'm here. It's my profession. I want to be a concert musician and the dizziness is working against me. I know I can be successful as a musician. I know I can play good music people will want to hear.

"I even have ideas for experimenting with classical music. I'm going to take the harmony of the spheres, the cosmic harmony, and translate it into music we use on earth. I want to let the divine inspiration of the universe flow through me when I play Bach or Beethoven."

"Have you played this way before?"

"I'm a failure when I play. I gave one recital and got one of these dizzy spells right in the middle of it. It was horrible. I couldn't concentrate on what I was playing and the results were disastrous. The reviews were so bad I'm ashamed to show them to anyone. But it wasn't me. It was the dizzy spells."

Now I had William stop and go back a bit to his earlier statements. This is something you can do at home, alone, when talking out a problem. The first comment he made was about his sex life and then he got into a discussion of his music.

"You said that in the beginning, your marriage was fine. Then you said that after a little time passed, it was more fun masturbating. Why is that?"

"My wife, Kathy, is very demanding. If she doesn't have an orgasm, she feels cheated. She puts a tremendous pressure on me to perform and that makes me nervous. When I get nervous, I figure to hell with it, who needs it? Besides, with my work, I'm in a position to meet a lot of pretty girls. Sometimes I'm able to vary my masturbation by taking on one of them."

"Do you feel the same pressure to perform when you have these affairs?"

"No. It's different because it's a casual encounter. The subject of performance never comes up. You never have to worry about orgasm. You get into bed, have sex, and probably never see the other person again."

"When did you first start having extramarital sex?"

"At the same time I started seeing Max. He's the doctor I went to for prescriptions to keep me calm and make me feel better. But he costs a fortune and that's why I left. It cost ten dollars a crack for each renewal and that's too much. I've got to find a way to get myself together without using crutches.

"Hey, you know, now that I think about it, maybe the

whole sex thing is somehow wrapped up with my failure at being a musician. Then again, I wasn't doing any good as a musician before I got married. I had the dizzy spells back then, too. I think, but they weren't as bad as after I got married."

"What about the pills you're taking? Did they have any effect on all this?"

"Not those, but I also get shots. In fact, I got my wife to get them too. They make you feel great; I mean, don't I look great to you even though I got all these problems?"

"Did you have a shot this morning?" I asked. I suspected he might have because it is unusual for someone to come to see me looking so apparently happy when he is actually extremely depressed. The drug could create that illusion.

"Yes, but how did you know?"

I suspected that the shot contained the stimulant amphetamine. There are a few doctors scattered around the country who use combinations of amphetamines, tranquilizers, and sleeping pills to get their patients through the day. It is totally improper and, in William's doctor's case, proved to be illegal. His doctor eventually went to court over what he was doing and lost his license to practice medicine.

"Tell me a little more about your sex life with your wife," I said.

"Kathy always expects an orgasm when we go to bed and it gets very tense for me. I don't always have the erection that I want to have. A few times I become impotent. Then she gets upset and says to me that I'm not doing anything for her. I tell her she isn't doing anything for me, either, and then we start to fight."

"Do you try to make love again when your tempers cool down?"

"Yes, but it's usually the same tense situation. We started having sex before we got married and we never had this problem. Everything was fine between us.

"Now Kathy quotes the women's-lib books a lot. I don't know whether I agree with it, though. I come from a conservative background. I think a woman has a certain place in the world."

William told me that he was talking of divorce and that Kathy was as anxious to save the marriage as he was. However, he saw no way out of their current dilemma.

I decided to wait to talk with William until I had talked with Kathy as well. They could just as easily have done this themselves, though. Each could have explained the situation as he or she saw it, then sat back and listened to the other speak. When you do this, neither party should interrupt. You should hear exactly what is being said by the other person, even if you don't like what you are hearing.

I also told William to give up his shots. I explained that I feared they were amphetamines and, since they were not given because of some sort of real illness but rather to affect his emotions and energy level, I felt they were unnecessary. I explained the details you have read in this book and he understood. He also was horrified.

"That's impossible," he said. "I've tried to give up the shots from time to time and it doesn't work. I get horrible withdrawal symptoms. I'm irritable and terribly on edge. My hands shake and I really can't afford to be in such a bad position."

I treated the injection withdrawal the same way I would any other drug addiction. I had him gradually withdraw, supplementing with the B complex vitamins, the choline, niacinamide, and dolomite for sleep. He used the choline heavily during the times he had withdrawal symptoms and this was especially helpful in controlling the cravings.

The following week, William returned with his wife. Both of them had been withdrawing from the shots, as I suggested. They were a little tired because they had slept less than usual that first few nights, but they were happy about living drug-free. The choline had handled their cravings, so they felt as though it was all worth the effort.

"Our marriage is a mess," said Kathy. She had pensive and earnest green eyes. "I know what William's health problems are, and they're the result of our marriage. He just won't admit that because he can't face the truth. That's why he's a failure as a pianist. It's all due to our marriage and he's too stubborn to admit the truth."

"What are your feelings about what is wrong with your marriage?" I asked.

"We don't have a decent sex life. We did, but we don't any more."

"Would you try to explain that to me a little, Kathy?" I asked.

> I guess it started when it seemed to me that he wasn't really making love to me. I know that sounds crazy, but his eyes were tightly closed all the time and it just wasn't a relaxing situation. It was as though he was thinking about someone else when he should have been enjoying me. It seemed to happen again and again until I suddenly realized how it was affecting me. I wasn't having orgasms any more.
>
> I told William I felt that he was using me for a masturbating machine. He got very uptight with me when I said that and lost his erection. I think that time, when I finally said what I was feeling, was the beginning of the end of our sex life. [Kathy looked at the floor, tears coming to her eyes. She was greatly upset, yet seemed simultaneously to be relieved to be expressing her feelings.]
>
> William said I was demanding things he couldn't give, that I was too much into women's lib. He started blaming the women's lib movement for everything, which is ridiculous. I believe in women's rights, but I believe in a man's rights, too.

Kathy repeated her story, stressing the sex-life problems she felt were the causes of their difficulty. She did not see the dizziness as a concern, even though that was why William had made the appointment originally.

My feelings after listening to each story was that the dizziness was a problem William created to avoid facing the real troubles. He was not being kept from being a pianist, nor was his sex life in danger, because of the dizziness. The real problem was the dysfunction in sexual relationship, a symptom of how they weren't sharing their every feeling.

As Kathy and William talked we all came to the same conclusions. Their problem involved both their sexual relations and Kathy's observation that William did not seem to be making love to her. The dizziness, which medical doctors had stressed was not related to any organic problems, had to be put aside in our thinking while these other areas were explored. I suspected that the real cause of all the problems was hidden in what William was thinking and doing at the time when Kathy felt he was not paying full attention to her.

William was more relaxed and happy during his next visit. He and Kathy were well into the program. His health was better, he was well rested, and he was reducing his use of drugs. He was anxious to clear up whatever negative thinking had affected his relationship with his wife.

"You told me during your last visit that your sex life was fine when you got married." I said.

"Yes, that's true. It was great. Kathy and I used to screw every night and sometimes in the morning, too. I enjoyed those days!" he said with a grin. "They were wonderful. I awakened each morning ready for action and most days she thought there was no reason to waste a perfectly good orootion. We had a wonderful sex life back then. We were very much in love and there was no women's lib in those days."

"Come now, William. There was women's lib back then, too."

"Yes, I suppose, but she wasn't into it as much as she is now. She goes to meetings every week. She reads all the books on the subject and she wants to have her orgasm all the time. She was never like that before."

"William, you are going to talk this through until you get to the bottom of whatever is affecting your relationship. You said it was good at first. When do you remember your sex life beginning to change in some way?"

William blushed and said, "I think it was the time when I almost had an affair. Don't get me wrong, I still loved Kathy and I didn't do anything, really.

"It all started when I met this gorgeous schoolteacher. She was one of these people who makes a major career change in order to feel better about herself. In her case, she was planning to become an entertainer, and you know that's in my line. I took her out to dinner a few times to talk about her plans and tell her what I knew about the entertainment business. Nothing went on at first, but I knew that she turned me on. She was gorgeous and we had a lot in common with our interest in the entertainment field."

"How did you feel when you made love to your wife during this time?"

"Actually I wasn't really thinking about my wife during that period. I was thinking about the schoolteacher. I would close my eyes and fantasize that I was on top of the other woman. I guess I was having my affair by using Kathy's body and my own fantasy."

"Was this during that period when Kathy says she felt you weren't really with her? Was this the time she described that she began losing some of her desire?"

"I never thought about it before, but I guess it must have been. Now that I think back, we had a fight or two and I worried that maybe I should feel a little guilty. But I hadn't cheated on Kathy, unless you call going out to dinner a couple of times doing something wrong.

"Anyway, we had a big argument and finally I really did turn to my friend for physical comfort. This time there was no fantasy. We had sex together and it was disappointing. Kathy was a much better lover and I realized that my mental image of the schoolteacher did not match the reality. I felt like a fool and was extremely guilt-ridden. Then I discovered that Kathy wasn't having orgasms with me and I felt even worse. Nothing was going right with my sex life and I knew I had almost hurt my marriage for an affair that was meaningless.

"It really wasn't the women's lib thing at all. I see that now. I focused on women's lib because that way I wouldn't have to face myself. I felt guilty about my one-night stand and took it out on Kathy. I yelled at her and called her a bitch. I was terrible."

"And that's when you began getting the dizzy spells?"

"Yes, that's the first time they started bothering me. Then my piano playing got worse and worse so I stopped practicing. I just couldn't practice without getting dizzy even though I had practiced seven or eight hours a day before that. I just stopped practicing and, even now, when I've taken it up again a bit, I don't do nearly the amount I should be doing. I'm overtired and my sex life is lousy. I've been depressed and I feel even worse than I did when I had the affair."

Slowly William's real problems were becoming clear to him. He was talking through his experience when he first had difficulty and he was seeing himself in a new light. He didn't like what he was seeing, yet through this self-understanding, he and I both knew that he could lift the horrible weight of guilt he was experiencing. He would be able to stop the dizzy spells with this new knowledge and we both realized that.

"I am beginning to understand things I didn't understand before," William admitted. "I can see why my marriage was failing. I can see why I sought everything from the tranquilizers to the amphetamines. I stopped playing the piano because I hated myself, then I hated myself more for stopping tho piano. I was creating all my own problems and trying to blame Kathy and the dizziness for what I was really avoiding within me."

Talking-it-out had a powerful result. William returned the following week with a bounce to his step and grin on his face. He was a happy man. "You know what I did after I left your office, Dr. Green? I took my wife out to dinner at one of our favorite restaurants. I also bought her a new necklace. I treated her as though we were courting and she loved it. We went home and both of us had the most satisfying sex we have had since I made the mistake of having that one-night stand.

"All week it's been like we were first married. We've made love morning and night and I've begun practicing the piano again. It was slow at first but I quickly regained the skills I had had and more. More important, I made contact with a booking agent and I have an audition for a possible tour as soon as I am ready."

That was several years ago. William went on to give extremely successful recitals in Chicago, Washington, Detroit, and several other major United States cities. He became popular enough to be asked to Europe for a tour. He has ten records on the market, an achievement he never thought would be possible. More important, his relationship with Kathy is successful and they have regained the kind of happiness they both thought had slipped away.

It is possible, by quieting your mind in meditation and going very deeply into the recesses of your inner being, to find answers for your problem on your own. This demands the highest maturity, wisdom, and insight, ingredients we don't always have when we need them. That's why a very important part of my plan is to find accepting individuals who will hear you out without trying to inject their opinions or being judgmental. You may find a "person" in a composite of sharings with friends, lover, spouse, co-workers, or anyone whose opinion you value and whose life you admire. You will also find that once you have verbalized your problem to several people it answers itself.

Some of my patients find that they like to utilize more than one listener for the specialized parts of their lives. They might like to talk about money and business with one individual, love and sex with a second person, and their concerns relating to health and recreation with a third. You may find certain friends have more expertise and success in these specialized areas.

Who should serve as confidant? Basically you want an open and accepting individual to whom you can speak freely and who can accept what you have to say. This should be someone who will let you talk through whatever is troubling you, pinpointing possible concerns you may be overlooking and giving you a different perspective on yourself.

Sex and money are two such difficult areas that we often suppress them. William did this with the dizzy spells. Others focus on minor or irrelevant concerns. Yet when talking aloud the real problem surfaces no matter how much you want to deny it.

There is never anything that can't be handled through

talking-it-out. Often with our love affairs, interpersonal relationships, and financial matters we do something about which we feel guilty. We suppress that memory and unconsciously create some problem for ourselves as a punishment. It might be in the form of a chronic depression or a stress-related illness. Once we understand the original incident through the process of talking-it-out, we also come to grips with what we had suppressed.

Before using a confidant to help talk out your problems, consider your personal attitude toward that person. Many individuals are raised to feel that certain matters for discussion belong exclusively with one sex or another. These are holdover sex roles from another time and circumstance. For example, some people feel that the opposite sex can understand their sex problems. A woman might be comfortable talking with a man and a man might be comfortable talking with a woman. In other cases, often involving money matters, both sexes feel more comfortable talking with men only.

I personally do not believe in limiting knowledge in certain areas to certain sexes because every individual has abilities and weaknesses based on unique characteristics unrelated to sex. However, if you do, be honest with yourself. Right now is not the time to try to change your sexual attitude. Right now is when you need to talk openly and honestly so you can find release from the pair that formerly drove you to tranquilizers and other drugs. You can work on what William called "women's lib" matters later. Right now you need to understand yourself through the assistance of someone you feel will make a good listener, regardless of whether or not that choice seems to be slightly sexist by other people's definitions.

Perhaps my most unusual case involving talking-it-out was that of Roger, a man of twenty-five who had one of the saddest faces I had ever seen. You could tell at a glance that he was extremely run-down despite his effort to keep up appearances with expensive clothing and a debonair manner.

Roger explained that he had once been a stockbroker, a wheeler and dealer on Wall Street. He had been very success-

ful for a while; then there began bad-investment problems
that gradually eroded his professional and financial standing. He had to leave his job and take a position as a clerk in a
stock brokerage company. It was a major step downward and
he wanted desperately to return to a position of success and
achievement.

Adding to Roger's problems was a potentially serious
mental illness. He hears voices and other sounds inside his
head. He talked of mental wanderings to Mars and the Moon.
He seemed paranoid and schizophrenic.

"Can you help me become successful again?" Roger asked
tearfully. "I want to be a stockbroker again but these voices
keep holding me back. I don't always know what's real and
what isn't.

"I've been going to a doctor for a while now. He's been
giving me vitamin B_{12} injections because I'm run down. He's
also concerned about the voices I'm hearing but can't find
anything really wrong with me. That's why he suggested I
come to you."

Another of Roger's problems was his conviction that his
doctor was trying to poison him with the injections. That
was the basis for his doctor's decision that Roger might be
paranoid.

"Why did you go to your doctor originally?" I asked,
trying to get Roger to talk through whatever might be
troubling him.

"I got into a bad way when my girlfriend threw me over for
another man. She did it right after I had business problems
and lost a lot of money. My business folded. I was extremely
depressed and thought I might need medical advice. But
things have been going downhill ever since."

I saw Roger as a man who considered himself a failure at
everything. He had lost his business, his money, and his girl,
the three most important aspects of his life right then. He
assumed his medical doctor didn't like him.

The doctor Roger was seeing was an honest professional. I
knew that the doctor's vitamin shots would not contain
anything additional which could be harmful. However, I also
felt that there was something more to his problem, and for
this Roger needed to talk about all those areas which might

be affecting him. I started with his diet on the chance that his real problem was hypoglycemia, always a prime consideration.

"Actually, I'm a health-food nut. I eat lots of fruit and vegetables—never junk stuff. I try to keep physically fit and I do meditation every day. I really am a great believer in a balanced existence of body and mind."

Still, nothing seemed right. It appeared that Roger was following all the precepts that would be beneficial for him. Perhaps he really was mentally disturbed in a serious way. I didn't know and felt we had to find out through talking. If he was just reacting to something in his personal life which he had suppressed, talking would uncover it for both of us.

"Roger, the only way either of us can understand you is for you to tell the whole story. You said everything seemed to go wrong about the time your girl broke up with you so let's go back to when you first were in love with her."

The relationship Roger described with his girlfriend, Hilda, seemed perfectly normal—at least at first.

> Then she met another man. I don't know when it was. I was so busy with the problems I was having at work that perhaps I overlooked obvious clues. I don't know. The first time I realized we were in trouble was when I arranged to meet her under the clock at the Biltmore Hotel. She never arrived.
>
> I called Hilda to ask where she was. I was worried, a little annoyed, but I never expected the answer she gave me. She said she had met a man named Peter and fallen desperately in love with him.
>
> But I need you, I told her. I said that she was my rock, my strength, and that my business was all going to hell. I begged her to be with me, but it was no use. She said she understood my problems but her love for Peter made it impossible for her to come to me. We were through and her only regret was the timing. She couldn't change her heart, she said. She couldn't leave Peter just because I needed her.

Part of the problem was that Roger knew Peter to be a great success in his work. "I didn't know where to turn, so I took a course to learn to meditate. I had a lot of time on my hands and I had had friends who meditated ten or fifteen minutes a day. They were always extremely refreshed and energetic afterwards so I figured that I could meditate four hours or more a day whenever possible, then conquer the world.

"I learned meditation and ever since then, I have been meditating five hours a day. I sit unmoving in a darkened room, my mind roaming free, yet it has not changed my life any. In fact, the voices started after that, so I guess I'm a little worse off than I thought. If it wasn't for the meditating five hours a day, I'd probably really be crazy."

"You meditate *five hours* a day?" I asked, shocked by what he had said.

"Yes. I started working three hours a day at meditation when I was still a stockbroker but as my business failed, I went to five. It kept me from being lonely without Hilda. I just wish I didn't have these voices now because they seem to keep me from getting anywhere."

"Roger," I said, trying to pick my words carefully so he would understand that, in his enthusiasm, he may have gone too far with his meditations, "everything has its limits."

Meditation is marvelous when handled for ten to twenty minutes a day. You can get alpha in seconds and do the theta exercises we discussed for a more positive life. But when you stretch meditation into three- and five-hour periods, you are isolating yourself in the quiet, without physical movement. Instead of the mind roaming free and your experiencing growth, you create an abnormal situation in which it is possible to become delusional—to hear your own thoughts and project them in your mind as somebody else's voices. What you are doing with your endless meditation is inviting mental derangement. Getting into alpha and theta for up to twenty minutes, twice a day, would be healthful and productive. Getting into alpha at times of crisis will be productive. But meditation for five hours at a stretch is actually *destructive* and has probably led to your current problems.

What I want you to do is to change your habits. I

want you to use the fractional relaxation techniques I have explained but I want you to do it only for the time I have mentioned. You need more sunlight. You need more exercise. Take a brisk walk with your free time and you will find that you get a natural high quite the opposite of the depression you have been feeling with your constant meditation.

I also want you to take more vitamins than I normally include in my plan because of the difficulty you have been having hearing voices. Dr. Linus Pauling, the scientist pioneer in Vitamin C research, has found that extra Vitamin C is extremely effective for mental problems involving perceptual changes. You have been hearing voices no one else hears and this is a problem with your auditory sense. Why don't you take an extra four tablets of a thousand milligrams each of Vitamin C spread throughout the day?

I also had Roger take Vitamin B complex and extra niacinamide. All three have been found to handle the problems Roger was experiencing and I felt he should try them. He understood about the chance of going to the bathroom with greater frequency and we discussed how he should alter the extra vitamins if he noticed that minor situation occurring.

Roger left my office slightly confused by what I had said, yet willing to try. He still had trouble believing that if twenty minutes of meditation once or twice a day was good, meditating for five hours wasn't that much better. He agreed that his way wasn't working and said he would try my approach even though I knew he feared that I might be wrong and he would get worse. He also agreed to the vitamins, though I think he was a little disappointed to not be getting a tranquilizer or some other "instant cure."

Roger returned the following week to begin talking out his feelings about Hilda. He seemed taller, healthier, and as handsome as the clothing he wore. He no longer stooped as he moved and, most important, the voices had stopped. His problem, as I suspected, was greatly overdoing the meditation to the point where it was truly destructive. Now it was time to find out the real trouble so he could fully resolve it.

Roger talked about his relationship with Hilda, concentrating on their breaking up. He said that losing her had hurt him but not nearly so much as the circumstances. He said that it was coming at the time when he was also losing his business that made the breakup so painful for him. He felt his pride and his male ego had been shattered by the experience.

Roger began to feel better as he talked. He understood that he had not faced the full emotional impact of his experience and this he was finally able to do through talking-it-out. He also discovered that when he cut his meditation time drastically, he actually found it more effective. He stopped being depressed and discovered he was gaining emotionally from the experience rather than becoming delusional from such extreme, needless and destructive sensory deprivation.

Next I told Roger about the exercises for entering theta. I showed him how to project a positive image in business. I showed him how to visualize his receiving the kind of work he wanted in order to change his negative programming. I also showed him how to visualize meeting a new woman, a woman who would provide him with all the love, understanding, and support he would need and for whom he could do the same.

There was no further need for Roger to come to my office. He was doing everything necessary to be a positive, happy, successful individual. He was moving forward and I wasn't surprised to hear his voice on the telephone several weeks later.

"Dr. Green, you can't believe how perfectly everything is working out. I met Julia about two weeks after I began visualizing meeting a woman I could truly love and share my life with. Actually, I had known her for quite some time but I had never paid any attention to her. She told me that she thought I didn't want a relationship because I always seemed to be signaling that I was unapproachable. I guess I was doing the reverse of what I learned to do through talking out my problems and properly meditating. In any case, I know she is the woman for me and she feels I am her perfect man. We're planning to be married and it is all because of you. Your methods really worked."

Roger's problem is not included to frighten you but rather to show you that even the best of plans can be abused.

Now a few years have passed and Roger is back to being a stockbroker again. He meditates fifteen minutes in the morning and ten minutes when he gets off work, has married and is watching his nutritional intake. His income is excellent and rising steadily, helping him to generate an increasing number of clients. He is taking the time to travel and is leaving for 4 weeks in Europe this summer. He always had the potential for success and now he is at least enjoying what had been just beyond his grasp.

Sometimes we are afraid to talk out our problems because we fear the ridicule which might follow. We decide that something is so horrible it simply cannot be discussed. Yet when we do talk it out, we find there is nothing wrong with what we are doing.

The fear of talking is commonly seen in the area of sexual fantasy. Contrary to what many people fear, there is nothing wrong with sexual fantasies so long as they do no harm and we are aware that they are fantasies. Some people enter the bedroom being pirates carrying off a wench. Others enter as Amazons who stand over throngs of aroused men, each begging to be taken by the Amazons' beautiful bodies. Still others are huddled against each other seeking warmth against a "snowstorm." The fantasies are numerous. Sometimes they are acted out with a willing, enjoying partner, and other times they remain inside our heads, increasing our sexual arousal. So long as both parties consent to the acting out and no one is hurt or turned off by the fantasies, they are perfectly normal. We all have them as they are a normal part of adult life.

Ed came to see me addicted to tranquilizers, $35,000 in debt to psychiatrists, and otherwise devastated by guilt over a sexual fantasy, guilt he never realized was needless. "I'm a bad man," Ed told me. "I'm a terrible man. For years I've done something awful with my wife and I'm embarrassed to talk about it. I've spent thousands of dollars for psychiatric treatment, thousands more for pills and I've even tried aversion therapy. None of that worked and now I'm hooked on tranquilizers and still doing this awful thing."

I braced myself. I felt certain that Ed was going to confess some secret sexual aberration. "What is it that's troubling you?" I asked. I first explained my plan for getting off tranquilizers, not because I felt that was the main priority but rather to put off hearing his story. I was certain I was going to be shocked in some way I didn't want to face.

"I . . . I. . . . When I get into bed with my wife . . . I fantasize that she is fourteen again. I've known her since we were teens and I picture her as a fourteen-year-old, beautiful virgin. I imagine that each time is the first and I am her seducer. I fantasize that she has never had sex before and I lead her into the best experience of her life."

I had braced myself for some grotesquely abnormal situation only to discover that Ed was enjoying a completely harmless fantasy. "Has your sex life suffered? Is your fantasy turning off your wife?"

She knows nothing about it. I've never had the nerve to tell her. We both enjoy making love regularly and I know I satisfy her. I figure she'd be horrified if she knew the truth.

I went to a psychiatrist about all this and he said that if I believed my fantasies were terrible, then I needed therapy to stop them. He said I would need years of psychoanalysis if I was ever going to be normal. I spent twenty-one thousand dollars with him and never got past age seven in our discussions. I finally realized he was just stringing me along. I knew I was troubled but I also knew I was giving him a weekly paycheck. He wouldn't even discuss my problem. He said that he needed to understand the root cause of my life before we could consider current problems and all I wanted to do was stop the fantasies. Then I went into aversion therapy. I sat in front of a screen with a device attached to me which gave me a mild jolt of electricity. The aversion therapist said my problems stemmed from fixating on teenaged nymphets. He said that I was horrible and a potential rapist. He used to flash pictures on a screen, showing me images of fourteen-year-old girls and giving me an electric shock each time.

But Dr. Green, I had no interest in teenage girls. My problem is the way I fantasize my wife when we go to bed together. I don't want to rape fourteen-year-olds. I find them all childish and completely unappealing. It is the fantasy with my wife which turns me on and I don't know what to do about it. All I've gained so far is less money in the bank and a tranquilizer habit.

To make matters worse, I used to have an advertising agency. I lost it, though, and now work for the people who bought me out when I was in deep trouble. I don't make much money any more and it is all because I'm so bad.

"Tell me about your advertising agency. How did your fantasy cost you that business?" I asked, I had the feeling that Ed was creating problems for himself due to his feelings of guilt when, in reality, the fantasy was harmless. I thought that if he talked through his recent life completely, he would fully understand himself.

I used to worry about my fantasy all the time. I would be told it was bad by the aversion therapist and I'd worry that I'd never get over it. All those years in therapy hadn't changed me, and the worst of it was that I didn't think I wanted to give it up. I was torn every which way and never had time for the business. I let my partner take over the accounting and he took advantage of my emotional state to begin embezzling money from me. Actually, my clients were very happy with my work. That's why I got offered a job from the firm which bought me out. I just couldn't pay the bills and that cost me the business.

Hey, I never thought about that! It wasn't my fantasy but my failure to keep control over the financial records. I let my partner have too much unchecked freedom. I wasn't being punished for fantasizing my wife as a virgin nymphet at fourteen. I may be bad, but that wasn't why I lost my business.

"Ed, I disagree with your definition of bad," I said, explaining about the normality of sexual fantasies. "You've been talking out your problems in my office and are seeing things in a new light. Why not go home and talk them out with your wife? She is just like everybody else, which means that she'll understand. You give it a try, then come back and tell me what happened."

The following week, a happy, bubbling Ed entered my office. "I don't know what your wife said but I suspect it was positive," I told him, delighted by his change in emotions.

Positive? Why, do you know she has her own fantasy about me when we make love? She told me that she fantasizes that she is a young virgin who is greatly aroused by me but who knows that she is not supposed to have me. Then I come along and speedily deflower her, just what she is hoping I will do.

Can you imagine? My own wife fantasizes just like I do and I never knew it. I thought it was something horrible. No one ever explained it was normal. I feel like such a fool, having to pick up the pieces of my life when I never did anything wrong or out of the ordinary. It is amazing how we can become a victim of those things we don't have the courage to talk about. You were right. Talking-it-out makes everything fall into place.

Ed borrowed the money needed to go back into business, this time starting a small office where he would have full control. His income quickly soared to over six figures and he is busily adding staff on a regular basis. He is doing well because he is quite skilled in this field and he is no longer needlessly troubled by past problems because he has managed to talk them out.

Fantasies are a part of you. They help to make you the whole person you are. They are not something to be feared but rather to be accepted. When you resist their reality they become monsters, preying on your mind, creating guilt and all manner of needless trauma.

Many fantasies are sexual in origin, and we feel needlessly guilty about these, when simply accepting them and enjoying them can free us from anxiety. In business we often have fantasies about future success, financial achievement, and personal prominence. Again, if we accept them as part of our working day and work toward those goals, both on the job and with the use of theta during meditation, they can become realities.

There is never anything so unspeakable in our lives that we can't face it. The problem is that we let our negative thinking create anxieties and fears. We compound the difficulty by letting doctors give us magic escape pills instead of facing what is troubling us. This continued repression eventually leads to a feeling that our lives are out of control. We magnify the problem until facing it fills us with terror. Some people stay heavily on tranquilizers and sleeping pills. Others become ill, fixing the blame on a physical problem, another person, or anything other than the real trouble.

Talking-it-out is the real magic pill. It is nonaddictive and its only side effects are peace, happiness, and contentment. When you talk out a situation, looking at it from a new viewpoint as you describe the experience aloud, you find the answers waiting inside you. You grow with the experience and learn new ways to view yourself and the world. You not only get off any drugs you may be taking, you also find that you never again have a craving for them. You are calm, enjoying yourself and life without using the crutch of pills to see you through the day. It is a wonderful feeling, and it all starts with just talking-it-out.

9

Exercise, the Cure
We Love to Hate

Many of you who are reading this book have arthritis, asthma, high blood pressure, ulcers, or some other stress-related problems. Your joints ache, you have chest pain, you tire easily or in some other way are afflicted with problems that have made you want to sit back, relax, and just try to get through life. You took tranquilizers and sleeping pills. Perhaps you ate "junk" convenience foods. You did every-thing you could to escape the problems, yet they never seemed to go away. Everything got worse and worse until you finally decided there must be a better way to live. That's why you bought this book, and now I want to explain the final part of my plan.

When most people speak of exercise they think of stren-uous activities like running or working out in a gym hour after hour. What they fail to realize is that taking the steps to your office instead of the elevator or parking your car a few blocks from work and walking the rest of the way in the morning sunlight is also exercise. More important, it is exercise that is not strenuous, yet gets your blood flowing and exposes you to natural vitamin D through photobiology (the science of the effect of light on the body and mind), and generally does exactly what you need to do for good health. The light receptors in the back of the eyes, receiving light, convert it to the Vitamin D that calms the nervous system.

I have told you how to stop taking tranquilizers, but this alone does not eliminate all the stress in your life. You still must face the problem that led you to seek the prescriptions in the first place. This is where exercise becomes a factor

The first reaction to stress is the flight-or-fight response, as we have noted. Adrenalin is produced in great quantity and we become tremendously anxious if we can neither act with violence nor run. When we rid our bodies of the adrenalin, either dissipating it throughout the blood stream or converting it to adrenochrome, we eliminate the feeling of stress that originally triggered our desire for the tranquilizer. Niacinamide converts adrenalin to adrenochrome, as we have seen. But we can't always take the vitamins we need at the moment we have a problem. An excellent course of action is to take a brisk walk—an activity that has been found to dissipate the adrenalin, spreading it so thoroughly throughout the body that we stop feeling the stress.

Vitamin D alleviates back pain because most back pain in aging individuals can be attributed to a mild case of osteoporosis. The bones have become weakened and fragile due to lack of the "sunshine vitamin." Cases of osteomalacia are also common among people who stay inside all day, exercising not at all or away from the healthful rays of the sun. In fact, the normal symptoms of early osteomalacia are general aches and pains. Patients complaining of such pains usually can't be precise because they feel bad all over, and this vagueness concerning symptoms prevents the diagnosis of a specific illness. The doctor may feel that the patient is a whiner or just having abnormal stress. A tranquilizer is the ideal prescription for malaise. The doctor may also tell the patient to get more rest, further removing the individual from the beneficial sunlight.

The heart is affected by inadequate Vitamin D. It can flutter and go into what is known as fibrillation in extreme circumstances. Unfortunately, doctors frequently prescribe nonessential pills and rest at such times. In many cases, however, if the patient would just take thirty minutes a day for a brisk walk in the sunshine, the Vitamin D naturally created would go a long way toward handling the problem. Needless to say, any regimen undertaken by someone who has symptoms of heart disease should be under the supervision of a physician.

One of the patients who benefited from the exercise portion of my plan was Mindy, a short, obese woman of over 200 pounds. She never thought she could benefit from exercise because she was always tired and sick. She had constant colds, migraine headaches, and had even spent time in a mental institution for what was reported to be schizo phrenia.

> I've been living in hell, Dr. Green [said Mindy]. I've taken amphetamines for my weight control, Valium for my nerves, Darvon for my headaches, and Thorazine in the hospital. I can't shake the depression and I can't lose any weight. In fact, the Thorazine just made me crave sweets all the more, and the hospital never restricted me because sweets are a lot easier, more popular and inexpensive for them than anything else.
>
> I've always hated myself. Even since I was a child I've felt that people were looking at me in a hostile way. I didn't want to live before I went into the hospital and I'm still not certain I do. Yet I'm only twenty-seven and I know I don't want to throw my body in the junk heap. I think the right thing for me is to go on without the drugs, without this weight problem, yet I don't know how.
>
> Can you help me?

Mindy was out of shape, yet the fact that she was ready for a change was the positive step we both needed in order for her to begin life anew. No one can get well unless he or she wants to get well. Once you make the decision to change, finding the best you can be within yourself is relatively easy. You have taken this positive step by buying this book and going on my plan. Mindy did it by coming to my office and expressing a desire for a new way to live.

Mindy told me about her unhappy childhood. Her father abandoned the family and her mother never forgave him for leaving them as he did. Eventually her mother developed cancer, but not before Mindy was having trouble with her weight and emotions. As her mother lay dying, she told Mindy that Mindy needed to get well, not let herself be killed by her father's abandonment the same way her mother was dying from her own unresolved emotions.

The first step in starting life anew is to abandon the drugs, as you have seen. Mindy went on my plan to rid herself of the dual dependency she still had. She was taking both Darvon and Valium heavily and was experiencing side effects from the drugs. The Valium seemed to increase her appetite, reduced her sex drive, and left her with a vague feeling of disorientation.

Reduced sex drive is a side effect of tranquilizers the pharmaceutical companies seldom report, seen in many of my patients. All tranquilizers, not just the Valium Mindy was taking, can reduce your sexual appetite. Some men have become temporarily impotent and all the heavy users I have seen have complained about this problem. In fact, a number of marriages have broken up as a result of this difficulty. The tranquilizers reduce the sex drive, then there are arguments in the bedroom leading to stress, which is handled through the taking of more tranquilizers—which further suppresses sexual ability.

The Darvon had its own side effects, compounding the problem. Mindy became drowsy from the Darvon but could not sleep at night. She then took Valium to handle the sleeplessness. However, Darvon in combination with tranquilizers can be quite dangerous and the manufacturer warns doctors of this fact on the information sheet included with the product and in the listing in the *Physician's Desk Reference*. Yet the doctor apparently was never concerned with this problem and continued prescribing both drugs for her as a matter of course.

Mindy was also taking Dexedrine for her weight, yet this is

a drug meant for very short-term use only, according to the manufacturer. She had tried to stop taking it from time to time, then found herself depressed and in need of more Valium, at least in her doctor's eyes. Yet the *PDR* listing for Dexedrine clearly stated some of the potential problems: "Abrupt cessation following prolonged high dosage administration results in extreme fatigue and mental depression; changes are also noted on the sleep EEG."

Dexedrine has the side effect of headache for some people, a fact which helped increase Mindy's use of the Darvon as a pain killer. It increased her insomnia despite the sleepiness, and this added to the problem. She then took more Valium to counter the drug.

None of the drugs was essential to Mindy's health. None of them handled more than the symptoms. Yet in combination, Mindy had become totally interdependent. Each worked against the other and increased the demand for them all. It was a nightmare merry-go-round traveling in a faster and faster circle while Mindy clung desperately to the horse, trying to keep from being flung outward and broken into pieces. The merry-go-round was traveling at a speed just short of being out of control when she entered my office. I worried that she might not be seeing me in time.

The drugs had also given Mindy the appearance of being schizophrenic, which is why she entered the hospital. The manufacturer of Dexedrine warns, for example, that psychotic episodes can occur with the drug, though it is rare when someone takes it in normal doses for the short term. It was the drug reaction, not true schizophrenia, which had caused her problems. Yet that did not change the fact that she had to go into an institution.

I decided to risk having Mindy gradually withdraw from all three drugs at the same time, doing it extremely slowly. The dosages of all of them were so high that I thought this could be done safely over a period of about six weeks. If she was doing it herself, I think I would have said to try just one drug at a time, taking longer for the full withdrawal. This was because I was able to monitor any problems which may have troubled her. There were none, as it turned out, but not being certain what might happen, I felt this was the best way. Doing it one at a time would have taken a few more weeks but would have been just as effective.

Mindy reduced her Valium by 5 mg per day for the first week, 5 mg more the second week, 5 mg more the third week, and so on through the six weeks it took to rid herself of the full 30-mg-per day dosage with which she had started. She also gave up a couple of milligrams of Darvon and an equal amount of Dexedrine in the same manner. As has always been stressed throughout this book, she made no effort to go "cold turkey." That would have been dangerous. Instead she went through the gradual withdrawal I always recommend.

"I was certain I was going to have problems," said Mindy when the six weeks were over. "I kept waiting for the hell to start and it never did. Every time I wanted a Valium, I took two thousand milligrams of niacinamide [the dose found most effective for her]. I took choline a thousand milligrams at a time when I had drug cravings and the cravings went away. I also found that I not only enjoyed the diet plan, I lost weight on it without being hungry. I feel as though I'm becoming a whole new person with the vitamins, the lack of drugs, and the meditation."

Mindy's metabolism was plagued by problems caused by her constant eating of sweets and the blood sugar variations that follows. She would get so hungry that she would swallow her food without chewing it properly. "It was a nervous reaction, I guess," she said. "I seemed to inhale it."

I explained to Mindy that it was important not only to increase the protein and fiber in her diet but also to chew her food adequately. It is through proper chewing that ptyalin, an enzyme in the saliva, can work in the manner in which it is most effective. The ptyalin helps digestion and eliminates the feeling of hunger. Gulping food instead of chewing it prevents this chemical reaction and increases the appetite regardless of the amount of food consumed, thus making overeating seem almost a necessity. Once Mindy began chewing her food at least ten times before swallowing, the ptyalin could work and digestion was handled in a way that did not result in constant hunger pangs.

Mindy found that she enjoyed changing her eating habits in order to lose weight. She had two eggs, orange juice, and herbal tea for breakfast. For lunch she had four ounces of protein in the form of fish, fowl, or lean meat. She had salad and a portion of fresh vegetables such as squash, celery, cucumber or cabbage, all watery vegetables that are both filling and low in calories. Dinner was basically the same type of meal as lunch.

The first four months of Mindy's diet resulted in a loss of almost forty pounds. Then she began having an occasional glass of white wine with her meals and an occasional slice of whole-wheat bread. She reduced her weight loss to a pound a week and even began enjoying such occasional treats as a piece of apple pie. Her appetite was reduced and her meals tasted delicious. She did not totally eliminate junk food after the first four months, but rather modified her diet so the occasional indulgence did her no harm. It was the kind of diet she found enjoyable to follow, not a chore.

Finally, after Mindy was off the drugs and into the change of diet for a while, I brought up exercise. Now Mindy was well aware that my plan worked. She was off drugs, happier and healthier than she had felt in years. She was painlessly losing weight and no longer craved the sweets around which she had once centered her life.

Do you think she enthusiastically embraced the idea of adding exercise to her regimen since she had seen that everything else worked? She hated the idea!

"I'm not an athlete. I get tired just going from one end of my apartment to the other. Some people were meant to live in sweatsuits and jogging togs. I was meant to live curled up by the fire with a good book. I'm feeling better. I meditate. I eat right. No way am I going to do something which serves no purpose other than to make the deodorant manufacturers rich!"

"Mindy, exercise need not be something horrible to experience, and I am not really suggesting that you drastically alter your lifestyle. Doctors have discovered that there are two types of fatigue people experience. One type is sheer physical exhaustion. It is the body's way of saying it has had enough exertion.

"There is a second kind of fatigue which actually masks the reality of the problem we are experiencing. It is not fatigue at all but rather a lack of physical exertion giving us the feeling of being tired. We feel weak, listless, like it is too much bother to do anything other than watch television or read. Yet this weakness is counteracted by exercise. If you go for a walk, go swimming, ride a stationary bicycle, or otherwise become active for a while, the fatigue magically disappears. We have new energy despite the fact that we have been feeling as though we are too tired to budge ourselves.

"I think that your tiredness is the result of too little activity. I also think the mild, lingering depression you occasionally experience could be countered by getting out in the sunlight. I want you to start getting at least three hours of exercise each week. I want you to spend perhaps a half hour each day taking a brisk walk in the open air. You can do it on your way to and from work. You can do it on your lunch break. I don't care how you do it, so long as you go out during the daylight.

"I'm not asking you to take up jogging because I don't think you will. I'm just asking you to walk rapidly for at least fifteen minutes at a time, twice a day, or thirty minutes a day all at once. I promise that you won't feel as though you're too tired to handle it. Try it for a week, then call me to tell me what is happening."

It was with great reluctance that Mindy took my advice. The first time she decided to try, she went for a swim when she thought she wanted to spend the day in bed. She knew that swimming in the indoor pool at the YWCA near her apartment was not getting sunlight but she felt it was the easiest way to test my theory about exercise countering most fatigue. When she climbed from the pool after taking several laps, she felt marvelously refreshed. She left the building and began walking along Manhattan's streets, moving more swiftly than she thought possible. The more she walked, the better she felt.

"I found myself singing after I had gone about a dozen blocks. People were turning to stare at me. I could almost hear them saying to themselves, 'Who is this nutty, fat broad singing along Broadway?' But I didn't care. I felt wonderfully alive. The traffic, the people, the dirt, none of it mattered. The world took on a special glow and I felt the kind of high I suspect drug users are forever expecting to encounter. It was a marvelous experience.

"When I took the subway back home, I suddenly realized that I no longer felt hostility coming from strangers. I used to hate the subway because I felt as though everyone disliked me. It was as if I was an outsider to the human race.

"Now that's not the case. I feel alive and a part of the world. Part of that was from the meditation exercises but much more was from the walking. I feel as though I have a new perspective on myself and others. I do belong to this world. I'm not worthless. I'm a part of life and it's a joyous feeling. In fact, my only fear now is that this good feeling might not last."

"Don't worry, Mindy. It does last. Daily exercise in the sunlight fills your body with the peace that comes from the natural creation of Vitamin D. Some experts have also found that joggers and walkers relax their minds and enter the alpha state, and you know how good for you that is. You just have to keep it up and the world is yours."

"But it's so easy, Dr. Green. I didn't get overheated or tired or anything. I just walked, enjoying the world. I moved quickly but it wasn't a pace that caused me to fight for breath like I've always feared with running. I've never felt so alive. My body feels great and my mind is so clear. I'm a totally different woman."

Mindy's learned to accomplish her work faster and more efficiently than ever before. She decided to take up jogging as a hobby, joining a club. "I never thought I'd see exercise as a pleasure. I still walk, but the jogging club has given me new friends, including a very special one. Dr. Green, I met Jim and he doesn't know that part of me I hated and abused for so many years. He just knows the person I am now and he finds me exciting. We're quite serious about each other and I suspect that it won't be too long before you get an invitation to our wedding. Your plan didn't just save my life, it's given me a whole new experience. Please tell your other patients exercise isn't the pain they think. Walking, alone, can help make you a totally new human being."

The people around Mindy did not change when she was on the subway. They were the same ones she perceived as being hostile before. However, when she changed her attitude toward life, she also saw the world for what it was. She was interested in others for the first time. She was open, loving, and ready to share life with those around. The people naturally responded in kind. This is something everyone who goes on my plan experiences because life is basically good without drugs. When we can see the world without the blinders of pharmaceuticals, we find that there is joy where once we felt only fear or depression.

My plan for getting off and staying off tranquilizers also helps cure illness. The exercise improves our circulation, strengthening the heart, the lungs, and the muscles of the body. Walking or jogging takes us into alpha and enables us to work out the problems of the day. Among my patients have been business executives with severe ulcers who are now completely well even though they eat a normal diet and are exposed to the same stress as before. One of these executives, the head of a chain of car-rental agencies and other service businesses, told me:

> I used to worry about the problems I had to face at work, the confrontations I would be experiencing with clients and staff. I would drive to work and feel the acid chewing at my guts. I'd grab the elevator to my office and arrive filled with tension. It would be one confrontation or crisis after another, business lunches and all manner of stresses I just couldn't avoid.
> Now I've changed all that. The stress factors are still there but I've learned how to handle them better. Instead of facing each day with my body tensed, I park my car in a garage a few blocks from my office. Then I walk from there, taking about fifteen minutes to cover the distance.

The first five minutes of that walk I'm usually pretty tense, then the rhythm of my pace, the warmth of the sun, and the relaxed breathing as I move begin to change all that. My mind begins to roam free. It is as though I am lifted from my body and I can think clearly again. I work out all the confrontations and the anticipated problems in my head. I decide how to handle that which I know I must face and then can relax until I must deal with something else.

I set my lunch appointments so I can walk to them as well. I am clear-headed when I arrive and clear-headed when I return, even if I indulge myself more than I should. Then, when the day is over, my walk back to the car enables me to resolve the troubles of the day. I again have everything in proper perspective and go home relaxed instead of remaining tense until a sleeping pill or tranquilizer can knock me out.

I haven't changed the stress I face at all, except for getting off the drugs I was taking. What I have changed is the way I handle stress. I don't compound it with tranquilizers and I use the walk to work out problems which otherwise seem to overwhelm me. I don't know if I believe in the existence of alpha the way you talk about but I do know that whatever happens, it is the best way to cope with stress I've ever encountered. And to think I always thought I had too many problems to even consider getting exercise.

With Mindy, the change was more than just the exercise. She used all the other aspects of the plan, of course. When talking out her problems, she found that she ate because she felt bad about the way she perceived her father hating her. She felt that she must be worth very little for the man not to want to have anything to do with her after he left the family, so she basically ate her troubles. Trips to the refrigerator were her way of avoiding the pain, even though the tremendous weight gain she experienced was placing a barrier in all her relationships.

Mindy also found that her headaches and much of the stress she was experiencing were caused by her high consumption of sugar. She was having mild hypoglycemic reactions because of the food, all of which stopped when she changed her diet.

There is another aspect to Mindy's story, an important one if you live in a city such as Cleveland, New York, Seattle, or any other place where rain and snow often darken the skies for days at a time. It is easy, under such circumstances, to not want to be bothered taking that walk. You have to bundle yourself up against the cold and the wet. You have to prepare to fight the elements. Your face stings and your eyes may run just stepping outside. It seems like a real nuisance and you may hate even considering it. However, Mindy did some experimenting using alternate forms of exercise as well as skipping all exercise on some of the worst days.

> I came to the conclusion that getting outside for a half an hour and just walking is worth it. Maybe some of the rays pass through the sky on days when the sun is hidden. Or maybe it's all in my mind. I don't know. I just know that when I stay inside, I always feel a little down by the end of the day. I'm always a little depressed. Sure, I hate getting wet and cold. The hardest thing in the world is opening the door to go out some days. But I don't get sick from the weather. My face may sting from the cold and my nose may redden, but I feel great when I come in.
>
> I do cheat a little. I bought myself an exercise bike to use on rotten days when I cut back my time outside to perhaps twenty minutes or a little more and I feel I still want to get more exercise. I've taught myself to read on the bike and occasionally I'll watch television from it. But I can't use the bike instead of the walk. There's something special about actually being outdoors, even though the weather is miserable. It's those times when I feel really alive, even though everyone else is hurrying to get inside.

Jill was another patient who was helped by the exercise portion of the program. A most beautiful woman with fashionably frizzed hair, a flawless figure, her radiant complexion surprised me because my tranquilizer users do not have such clear skin. However, Jill also wore an aura of depression. The way she stood, talked, or sat seemed to radiate intense sadness.

"I have an ulcer, Dr. Green. That's the cause of all my troubles. I went to a shrink for a while but he wasn't much help. I tried a doctor who put me on a milk diet and that didn't do anything but give me diarrhea half the week. Finally he decided that what I really needed was Valium."

I would have liked to have been shocked by what Jill was telling me. The idea that someone would prescribe Valium for an ulcer patient seems horrible to me even though I understand the theory behind it. Valium is meant to handle stress. It is prescribed to ease feelings of anxiety, the kind of emotions which can lead to ulcer development. But Valium does not alter a person's way of thinking. It does not teach us how to cope with life. All it does is mask our anxiety. Unfortunately, masking reality is not going to change it or teach us how to deal with it. That is why it also will not help us overcome the basic cause of an ulcer.

What Jill needed to know were some natural alternatives. Zinc is a vital mineral for shrinking ulcers as it is crucial for the enzyme system to operate properly. Enzymes are boosters that speed up chemical reactions in the body. There are more than eighty zinc-containing enzymes. Jill could get her needed zinc by emphasizing in her diet her choice of the following foods: organ meats, whole-grain bread, chicken and turkey, walnuts, and especially oysters.

"I know what the doctor wanted. He figured if he could suppress all my worries, I'd get better. It sure didn't work that way. My stomach hurts like hell and now I can't seem to quit taking the tranquilizers without really freaking out. I've been on them for three years now and I think it's time I tried something else. You're probably as bad as everybody else but when you feel like I do, what've you got to lose except another lunch?" Jill laughed at her half-hearted attempt at humor, then looked dour again. She was a miserable woman who had the beauty and intelligence to succeed at anything she tried. Yet she was almost ready to give up on life.

I placed Jill on the plan and, as usual, she was not allowed to go cold turkey but had to cut back very slowly, extending the withdrawal period over several weeks. I explained the role of zinc in shrinking ulcers and told her to take it in conjunction with Vitamin B_6, Vitamin B complex, and pantothenic acid. I also prescribed fractional relaxation—relaxing all parts of the body to quiet the mind.

"I also take a nose spray. I have asthma and I must use the spray three or four times a day when I am being affected by allergies, pollen, air pollution, and all the other crud that makes Manhattan so beautiful. I can keep using that, can't I?"

"It's not essential for your health any more than the Valium, is it? It gives you comfort but it doesn't cure anything or stop anything, does it?"

"Not really. But what if I have an attack? It does help me to breathe easier even if the chemical is giving me stress like you've told me."

"Let's compromise, Jill. You carry that spray but use it only when you feel it is an emergency. I want you to use a different kind of medication for your asthma, a natural medication which I think you will find works better than any pharmaceutical ever invented. You carry that nose spray but I am going to have you use Vitamin C to control your asthma."

"You're nuts, Dr. Green. I mean, pardon my language but what you're saying can't be true. I've been to three other doctors and not one has mentioned Vitamin C. You want me to drink an extra glass of orange juice in the morning or something?"

"Not exactly. I want you to use large doses of Vitamin C to handle your problem. I know the other doctors never suggested it—but they didn't get you well, either. All I ask is that you give my program a try. I've got too much of a reputation at stake to want to do something that might harm you or prove meaningless. I want to be able to brag about my curing you and I couldn't if my methods didn't work."

"All right. That does make sense," she laughed.

"Your nose spray contains cortisone and that has a number of bad side effects. Not only does the chemical cause stress, it also has the side effect of destroying much of the Vitamin C you've already taken naturally in your food. You're getting stress and the few benefits of good nutrition you may have had are being overwhelmed by the loss of Vitamin C. Stopping the nose spray except when you feel you absolutely must have it and starting to take extra Vitamin C will change your entire situation."

I also had Jill take extra Vitamin B complex (100-mg tablets) and extra Vitamin E (1200 IU when a woman normally needs between 600 and 800 IU). I explained that most of the vitamin quantities were not meant for the long term but rather for use during the period when she was getting off pharmaceuticals and stabilizing her body.

"You are also going to need to exercise as part of this program," I said.

"Are you trying to kill me? Do you know what it's like getting out and breathing the crud in the air? I react to everything."

"You're not going to die, Jill. Quite the opposite. I think that you will find that with the vitamins you are taking, as you begin to walk or jog, you will actually feel better, not worse. There may be some mild discomfort at first but nothing serious. I don't want you running the marathon through a field full of pollen. I just want you to take a half an hour a day, perhaps in two fifteen-minute segments, and walk around the block, through the downtown area, in a park, or anywhere else you might enjoy.

"All I ask is that you try. Where are you currently living?"

"With my mother," she replied disgustedly.

"How do you feel about that?"

"Terrible. I hate living with her."

"Then why live with her if you hate it? You're an adult with a good job. Why not get your own place in the city?"

"She's all by herself. How will she manage if I don't live with her?"

"Can you employ someone to look after her?"

"Of course. Money isn't a problem for mother. She owns two large apartment buildings in New York and has a chauffeur for her car."

"Then there's no reason you can't afford to get an apartment in the city on your own."

"No problem. In fact, my mother's real estate firm will cover the cost."

"Good. Then why don't you do just that? You want to get rid of your ulcer and your asthma. The first step is to stop poisoning your body with the chemicals of needless pharma-ceuticals; the second step is to change your lifestyle. You obviously don't enjoy living with your mother, so why continue subjecting yourself to the stress of such a relation-ship when you have just proved to yourself it is needless?"

The more we talked, the more I realized the kind of hell to which Jill had been subjecting herself. She hated her mother and the constant nagging she received. She would spend as much time away from home as possible, grabbing a dough-nut here, a hot dog there; coffee, sweet rolls, anything she could get. Her nutrition was terrible and she was being mentally poisoned by the stress of her nagging mother. Her life with the older woman was a constant battle.

Jill realized she had a choice. She moved out of her mother's home and into an apartment when she started my plan. She got a volunteer job at an area museum to help maintain her interest in the world around her. She also began withdrawing from Valium, adding extra zinc to her vitamin regime since zinc is a mineral with special benefits for getting rid of ulcers. Zinc is vital for proper insulin functioning and the utilization of carbohydrates, the two main problems for hypoglycemiacs.

Three weeks into the plan, accompanied by an extra 200 mg of zinc, making a 300-mg total, Jill realized that she looked and felt better than she had in months. She even felt less stomach pain, something which surprised her. She decided to have her stomach X-rayed to see if there was any change or if it was a case of just having her feel so good that she imagined everything to be perfect. To her delight, the ulcer was shrinking.

Jill began walking the six blocks from her apartment to the museum, curious about how the exercise would affect her. She was uncomfortable the first few days. It was cold in the city and the wind whipped about the sidewalks surrounding New York's skyscrapers like a minihurricane. Her lungs burned slightly and she felt a tightness in her chest. She was taking extra Vitamin C and, though she reached for her purse several times, she discovered she didn't really need her nose spray. She came close to using it, and once started to panic over the way she was feeling. Yet, to her surprise, she got along without it.

By the end of the first week, Jill told me that she was having no trouble with the walking. She was going much faster and neither the wind nor the whirling dirt caught in the vortex of the wind affected her breathing. In fact, she decided to begin leaving her apartment in the wrong direction at first to add distance to her walk.

Jill was not just walking, she was practically flying within two months. She started wearing a good pair of tennis shoes, packing her heels in a bag for when she got to the museum. Then she would "rove," a term she used to describe a combination of walking and jogging. She would walk briskly, then break into a run for the sheer joy of it, then slow to a walk when she got a little tired. Her smile seemed permanently etched across her face and the heads of enchanted males were constantly turning to watch her as she passed.

Then, to my surprise, Jill brought Ben to see me. Ben was a handsome young attorney who was on the board of the museum where Jill worked as a volunteer. They were totally enamored of each other, but Jill worried about Ben's self-image. He was in a highly stressful job to which he had never adjusted. He didn't feel worthy of his situation and his success in life, and he had difficulty sleeping. He had begun to take Equanil, a minor tranquilizer used to counter anxiety as well as being given as an aid to sleep. However, he quickly became psychologically dependent upon the drug.

One day Ben discovered that he was over-reacting to the medication. He went to his doctor complaining of slurred speech and constant drowsiness. The doctor promptly switched him to Triaval, a much stronger tranquilizer designed for use by people who are both anxious and depressed. It is a very powerful drug, much stronger than Equanil.

Ben reacted to the Triavil by getting a rash at the dosage his doctor initially recommended. He was told to cut back, but when he did, he regained his depression. It seemed to be a choice of feeling miserable or breaking out, neither of which was pleasant.

Jill explained my program and convinced Ben to try it. They also began jogging together every morning, watching the sun rise in the sky, moving along the sidewalk and through the park side by side, oblivious to the world.

At the end of the six weeks, Ben was free of drugs and delighted with his new health. He felt marvelous and both he and Jill greatly reduced their vitamin supplements because the exercise, meditation, and diet changes were handling their anxieties. Ben continued to use niacinamide heavily during periods of high-stress, relaxing in the knowledge that any excess would pass harmlessly from his body. However, the one stress situation he handled without any help at all was the day he proposed to Jill. As I write this, their baby has just celebrated his first birthday and they are very happy together.

Tammy was a woman who felt it was impossible to implement my plan. She had four children, all of them under six. Her husband worked long hours and she was left to handle the screaming and yelling. "Maybe your program does work but people like me can never stick to it. We have too much to do. Taking a Librium is the best way for us."

The answer for Tammy was a simple one and may be perfect for you if you are also having problems with your time and family matters. I knew that there was no way she could meditate while listening to the noise of the radio and television, the happy squeals of children at play. I told her to take earplugs, go into a room and shut the door when she knew the children were safe in the play area. Then she should meditate that way, the noise blocked out artificially for ten to twenty minutes. Whenever she felt that the older child would not watch the younger ones, a situation which usually occurred, she had a neighbor friend who could step in and watch the children. In fact, the neighbor was so interested in my plan that they began sitting for one another during the exercise times.

Exercise can be as simple as parking farther from work and walking the difference. It does not have to cause you to smell like a gym locker right after high school football practice. Exercise means getting your heart and lungs working more efficiently in the daylight, and this can be done at a pace that is comfortable for everyone.

I follow the plan outlined in this book because it gives me pleasure to do so. The "right" foods also happen to taste good! Vitamins can be taken in a matter of seconds each morning. The exercise entails walking a few blocks to and from work daily and jogging on weekends. I meditate in the morning and in between patients when my schedule is light. I talk things out with my wife and with dear friends.

Living a tranquilizer-free existence is delightful. It is a positive way to live and live well. You need no saffron robes, no special mantra, no macrobiotic diet or pilgrimage to a guru. In fact, most of your friends will be unaware that you have changed your lifestyle much at all, except for the fact that you are happier and healthier than you have ever been.

10

The Joy of Life
Free from
Tranquilizers

Congratulations! You have made it. If you have followed the program described in the preceding chapters you should now be living free from tranquilizers, sleeping pills, and antidepressants. You are in control of your life. You have taken your time, in order to avoid withdrawal complications. Choline has handled your cravings during the stressful period of withdrawal, and dolomite, niacinamide, and L-tryptophane have ensured restful sleep. You look better, you feel better, and—best of all—you have a more relaxed perspective on life.

I am as pleased for your present happiness as if you were one of the clients I see every day in my office.

Maybe you are a little afraid to say this to your family and friends now that you have come so far, but if you are like many of my clients, you may be somewhat uneasy about what the future holds. What happens when your life is *not* filled with so much joy as you may be feeling at this moment? What will you do when your life takes a temporary twist in a direction that is unpleasant? How will you react to stress in the future? Will you want to return to the very drugs you fought so hard to escape?

Or suppose you have never experienced the hell that dependency on tranquilizing drugs can become. Perhaps you purchased this book not because of your problems but because of the problems of loved ones. You want to help someone else who has insomnia, physical discomfort, or extreme emotion. You want to help him or her resist all present and future recourse to tranquilizers, sleeping pills, and antidepressants. You can! This plan works!

It is impossible for me to predict what stress will come into your life; stresses vary with individuals. The death of a loved one, a divorce, or the loss of a job can cause extreme emotional upset. Even positive stress has to be adjusted to. Marriage, promotions, childbirth, and moving to a new home also require mental and physical adaptation.

No two people are likely to experience stress the same way. Perhaps you love to sit in rush-hour traffic, playing "bumper tag" as an endless line of cars attempts to advance along the jammed freeways, whereas some might come close to panic under such circumstances. Others would rather walk ten miles than get behind the wheel of a car at such times.

I listen to individuals' troubles all day, delighting to help them find new insights. I find no stress in such work, although people often ask how I can endure to hear anguish for forty hours a week.

The stress may show itself through an upset stomach, lack of appetite, or overeating. You might bite your nails or yell at the slightest provocation. Or you might develop the stress reactions that manifest themselves as cancer, asthma, diabetes, arthritis, or allergic reactions. We may focus on these symptoms to avoid facing the problems with which we need to learn to live.

One woman who came to me to learn my plan for living without drugs, Alice, had endured the most inhumane treatment currently used in the United States—electroshock. This barbarous treatment involves creating an artificial convulsion with electric current. No one knows exactly what it does or why some patients seem to feel better afterward. Nor does anyone know why some patients do worse, experiencing short and long-term memory loss, insomnia, and numerous other difficulties. It is a type of treatment so unpredictable that it has been outlawed in many Western European countries, yet it is still in use in some mental hospitals in the United States.

Alice was diagnosed "psychotic." She was placed in a mental hospital, and after electroshock treatments had great difficulty remembering.

"I'm a schoolteacher, Dr. Green," said Alice, who was in her early forties when she came to see me. "I guess my problem started when I went out with this man. I fell in love with him, hopelessly in love with him. He was younger than I was, handsome and so full of life! He told me that we were going to get married and I was very happy. And then he seduced me."

Alice bowed her head and started to cry. She wept bitterly with the memory, as though her story was the most torturous nightmare anyone could endure, even though I had heard similar stories many times before.

> I am a devout Catholic and I believe in being a virgin before marriage. He was the first man I had ever had sex with and it just seemed so right at the time; I was certain he would marry me and everything would be all right. But he abandoned me. Seduced and abandoned. It sounds like something out of a bad novel. But it happened and I went into a depression. I felt like I was in a bottomless pit, dropping into Hell while huge boulders were tumbled down the opening above me so I could never climb back out.
>
> My medical doctor didn't know what to do with me. I was ashamed to talk about what happened but it wouldn't have mattered anyway. He was a Catholic too, and his beliefs were like mine. He would have been disgusted with me, just as I was disgusted with myself. He told me the only hope was to go to a private institution, which is where they gave me electroshock treatment.
>
> After the electroshock treatment, my memory was ruined. I remembered nothing and only now have

vague memories of all that happened. I complained about this to the doctor at the sanitarium but he just laughed. He said that was the point. I was overwhelmed by guilt, and if I couldn't remember everything, I would start to feel better.

It was so stupid of him, Dr. Green! It wasn't that I couldn't remember just my love affair. I'm a schoolteacher and I can't remember how to do arithmetic. I can't remember the things I used to teach. I can't remember anything. There are so many gaps in my memory of my past education there seems to be no way I can make a living. How can I teach history if I can't remember history? How can I teach math if I can't remember math? I worry constantly and I can't sleep at night. The tranquilizers they prescribed don't help. The sleeping pills don't help. Nothing helps.

I explained my plan to Alice and she began trying it. I knew that the sleeping pills were actually the cause of her sleeplessness and it took her less than a week of following my vitamin regimen before she knew it, too. The B complex vitamins, niacinamide, dolomite, L-tryptophane and the others all worked to break her destructive pattern. She began to rest at night, then to sleep so deeply and totally that she awakened feeling better than she had since the nightmare of her affair.

Next Alice began talking out what happened. She described the affair over and over again, adding more details to her conscious mind each time. The more she told her story, the more she could remember. Sometimes it was just the name of a restaurant where they had eaten. Other times it was what he had said to try to get her into bed. But what she said during one session she retained through the next, adding details. Her memory was coming back and the vitamins, the choline, and the other parts of the plan were helping her to regain abilities lost to the shock treatment.

I went through eighty sessions with Alice. She repeated her story over and over because her brain had been so badly damaged by the electroshock treatments. She eventually triumphed on my plan when all else had failed.

"I remember something else, too. I remember the blueness of his eyes. I told you before that David had brown eyes, but they weren't brown, they were blue. I can remember him so vividly that I can see his eyes clearly, and they are blue. And I also remember . . . I remember . . ." Alice began to cry.

"What is it?" I said, knowing she had touched upon a subject so painful for her that it might be a cause of her depression. "Remember and say it aloud and you will be well."

"I know. I just don't want to talk about it. You see, I remember that David needed five thousand dollars and I gave it to him. I gave him five thousand dollars and then never saw him again. Now that I think back on it, he used me. Every time we went out to dinner, I took the bill and I paid it. You know, I just realized something I never faced before."

"What's that?" I asked.

"David was a gigolo who took advantage of me. I never could say that to you when I first came to see you. I never could speak badly of him, even though he deserved it. He used me and I felt badly.

"You know, by saying what should have been obvious right from the start, I feel like a new person. I've been sleeping at night for quite some time. I'm not taking any pills. And now that I've admitted to myself exactly what David really was, I can accept the fact that it's past. That part of my life is finally all behind me.

"I'm going to stop acting the way I have been. I'm going out to find a new relationship. There are plenty of men in the world who are decent, warm, and beautiful. I have a lot to offer and I am no longer so filled with self-hate that I will refuse to spot a man who is trying to use me."

Alice's recovery was gradual. The B vitamins, particularly choline and B_6, along with exercise, meditation, and talking-it-out, gradually restored her memory. Choline's efficacy for memory has recently been demonstrated. 500 milligrams of choline is contained in 1 teaspoon of lecithin, mentioned in my food-supplement drink to be taken in the morning. The harm Alice experienced was severe enough that, to this day, we are not certain it is 100 percent restored, but she is teaching again and, if there are lapses, they are so unimportant as to get overlooked. She also began dating again and eventually found a man whom she felt was perfect for her. Almost two years after Alice walked with confidence from my office, I received a wedding invitation from her. She had learned to handle stress constructively and had overcome the damage done by unthinking medical professionals.

All of us encounter hostile people in positions of authority. We must deal with defensive people who project their problems on everyone around them. And then there are the simple but anxiety-producing crises of everyday life. Our plumbing breaks down when we are expecting guests, people get sick when we are counting on them. We get stuck in traffic jams or our car fails to start when we are late for an important appointment. These are stresses we can neither anticipate nor avoid. It is obvious from your past experience that taking a tranquilizer is the worst way to gain control over your emotional reactions to stress. But how should you plan for the unpredictable upsets of daily life?

The first step is to try to place the problem in full perspective by analyzing all sides of the matter. The traffic jam is a good example. Your normal reaction is likely to be panic because you are going to be late for an important meeting. This is one facet of the problem. However, by controlling your fear and seeing other sides, you will realize that: (1) You are helpless. You cannot change the reality of the traffic jam. (2) Eventually the police will arrive to handle the problem and you will be able to drive on. (3) A call to the party you are meeting and an honest explanation should bring understanding. Everyone has experienced traffic jams. Most people are sympathetic when they know the truth and will reschedule the meeting. (4) If the other party involved is unrealistic and refuses to "hear" your explanation, there is nothing you can do about it. (In fact, you may conclude that you don't really want to do business with such a person.)

Sometimes the problem is one we must face but one that causes us great anxiety. The end of a relationship is one such example. Once you understand what you must do and why, try using exercise and meditation to resolve all the issues you currently fear to face.

Go for a walk or a jog in the sunlight. Move rapidly and with purpose. Let your mind run free, thoughts of your problem drifting by. This is not the time to try and hold them. Let them move like passing clouds as you try to clear your mind, much as you would for meditation.

After a few minutes you will find that you are shifting into alpha, and that is when you will begin thinking about the problem in earnest. Now stop those thoughts, looking at the problem from all possible angles, weighing alternative solutions. If you still feel overwhelmed, think about people with whom you can discuss the matter for a different perspective. If it is a financial matter relating to your business, perhaps your comptroller or an independent accountant will be the answer. If it is a personal problem, perhaps you have a friend within the company or someone in a related business who has had the same experience and can offer you suggestions.

Dr. Hans Selye, an expert on handling stress, points out that the benefits of physical exercise go beyond the physical. If you are at one with the movements of your body and increasing the amount of oxygen to the brain, obsessive, top-of-the-mind thoughts fall by the wayside. It is virtually impossible to exercise and worry at the same time. I'm sure you've had the experience that anxieties seem less important or nonexistent after a fulfilling walk or job outdoors. In fact, it's a perfect way to get an expanded view when you are thinking through a problem.

Next use visualization. Create a picture in front of you in which you are being happy, free of tranquilizers, joyous. If you have trouble conjuring a specific image, just concentrate on capturing the idea. Make the visualization as real as possible and draw it into you until you feel it becomes a part of you. Pull it into you, in front of your body, to the left of your body, the right of your body, above your body, below your body, behind your body. This technique can be effective in dealing with such large adjustments as death or divorce, or retirement.

Finally, talk out the matter with a confidant. When you've determined what both your intuition and your logic indicate is the strongest path to follow, have the courage to take this course of action indicated by your research. Convert your words to immediate action. Waiting for tomorrow will only make today's pain and previous indecision hurt more. Taking a tranquilizer or other nonessential medication just delays the action. You avoid facing the trouble which you know in your subconscious is always lurking to haunt you. Fear builds out of proportion to reality.

I have repeatedly stressed walking during daylight for your exercise because this is one activity everyone can do. It does not matter where you live, what the weather is like, your age or physical condition.

Walk as rapidly as is comfortable, gradually increasing your pace every few weeks until you find a speed that is truly making your heart and lungs work effectively. This is the concept behind aerobic exercise, which was developed a number of years ago. You might be interested in checking your library or paperback book stand for books such as Kenneth Cooper's *The New Aerobics* to better understand this concept.

Jogging, which is actually a slow run, can cause harm to your knees, kidneys, and other parts of the body if done improperly. However, it is one of the more popular sports today and one in which you may wish to indulge a part of this program. Before starting to jog, read up on the exercise to learn about proper shoes and jogging surfaces. Sidewalk jogging may damage the knees or kidneys. Jogging on grass or sand is better but may not be possible where you live. You should also follow the ten important points:

1. Get a health check-up before you start jogging. See your medical doctor for a complete physical regardless of whether you are eighteen or eighty. Our sedentary lifestyle and improper diet has created a situation where some teenagers have early hardening of the arteries and occasional heart attacks. Youth doesn't guarantee good health. Physical activity and diet can make a retiree in better physical shape than his or her great-grandson

2. Buy proper shoes fitted for your feet. Cheap running shoes purchased in a discount store might not have proper support. Also, a shoe which is meant for walking or tennis may not be designed for jogging.

3. Eat yogurt or yogurt with fresh fruit (no sugar or variations such as corn syrup) before jogging to give you energy. This is a good idea before a long, rapid walk as well. Take fluids so you won't dehydrate.

4. Do not try to jog heavily at first. The first few days or weeks should involve a combination of walking and jogging. You want to walk, jog, walk, jog in a pattern which allows for gradually increasing the period you jog and decreasing the time you walk.

5. Combine jogging and meditation. Breathe in deeply, then exhale with a ten count and breathe in deeply again, repeating the cycle.

6. Don't compete with others. Jog for the joy of it and the mental benefits. Jog for the physical conditioning which results. But don't jog to beat someone else, because this is destructive. Jogging should be a tool for self-improvement and gaining control over your life, not a competition.

7. Don't try to pass the person in front.

8. Don't show off either in the way you jog or the distance you try to achieve. Work toward what is best for you.

9. Do stretching exercises and walk around, both before you start and after you are done.

10. Always try to jog in the sunlight and open air. Jog outdoors even when the skies are overcast.

George, a man in his early forties, thought he was going through midlife crisis. In fact, he was just being overwhelmed by stress compounded by a lack of exposure to natural light.

"I've got to get away," said George, sitting in my office at the request of his wife. She felt that their marriage was in danger because of his extreme emotional state. She hoped there might be a less drastic solution than the one he wanted to take. "I want to go to California."

"I know just how I'm going to do it. I'm going to shack up with a young girl at Big Sur. I'll sell everything I own and give my wife the money. She'll be set for life and I can go out and live on the beach. I'll smoke a few joints and be a hippie. Maybe I'll go to one of those encounter groups and freak out with the rest of them. I don't care what I do so long as it's different. I want to live! I want to be free!"

"Your wife thinks you've already started," I told George. "She thinks you've found another woman and that's the person you're going to live with."

"Another woman? That's nonsense. Colleen's been the perfect wife. It's not her. It's me. Maybe I'll come back in a few years if she still wants me, but maybe I'll be too changed, too free to ever return. I wouldn't look for anyone else until I got out there, but I just know I'll find someone. I don't want to live there alone. I just want to be there. I want to go and be free, free, free! And don't tell me you're going to try and talk me out of this, because I know what's best for me!"

"No, George, I'm not going to try to talk you out of anything. I just want to help you find perspective. I think I have an idea what the problem you're reacting to might be. You have a lot of stress in your life and you're having trouble handling it, aren't you?"

"That's very true. I'm not handling the stress well. That's why I need to go to California and start a totally different life."

"Yes, your approach is to turn your back on your life. You want to go somewhere new, where the old problems don't exist. Many of my patients take tranquilizers to try to get away. You want to go to California."

"I guess that's one way of looking at it. You're right."

George was a busy executive, he arrived at the office early and stayed late. He was financially successful, despite his emotional condition. I suspected his problem had to do with the way he lived indoors and I decided to question him about this. "Tell me, George. How much light do you get every day?"

"Are you crazy? What does that have to do with my job and homelife pressures?"

George went on to describe the normal suburban commuter's life. Most of the year it was dark when he got up in the morning. He dressed in the dark, drove to work in the dark, then entered a world of artificial light. There were windows in his office but, by the time the rays had filtered through the tinted glass, their value was reduced to almost nothing. If he left late, the sun was down and it was dark again. Even leaving at a reasonable hour made him drive in near darkness so he never really felt the light. Then, when he got home, he and his wife would spend time in front of the television set, again missing any sort of daylight.

"What really attracts you to California, George? Is it the beautiful women who live there? Is it the freedom from your wife and children? Is it the light and the beach? Tell me what is most appealing for you?"

"I have this fantasy. I see myself lying on the beach with the sun beginning to lower. The waves are lapping in front of me and the seagulls are flying overhead. My whole body is warmed by the sunlight. I feel the rays penetrating my skin. It is almost blinding in its intensity, yet I feel no fear. The light is my friend. The light is . . .

"I think you've hit on something. I'm thinking about sunlight. I'm actually craving that sunlight. I never thought about this before, but I think my desire for the sunlight is the strongest motivation I have right now."

"George, I want to try a fantasy game with you for a moment. It may seem silly but I think it may also provide a new possibility for your life. I want you to close your eyes and picture yourself in the country. Upstate New York has large areas of beautiful wheatfields and I want you to mentally transport yourself there. You can sit on a grassy slope overlooking the fields or lay down right in the middle of them. Just put yourself there in any way that is comfortable. The sun is shining and its warmth and light are penetrating your body. You are comfortable and at peace, basking in the warmth of the sunlight. You know you are thousands of miles from California but you are feeling the sun in the middle of this field. Are you getting the image?"

"Yes, and it's wonderful. I feel just as calm and content as if I were in California. It's the sun I want. It's definitely the sun."

"That's what I thought, George. I'm not going to tell you what to do with your life. I'm not going to tell you not to go to California and start over. But before you sell everything and leave your family, there's one thing I want you to try. I want you to start jogging or walking briskly each day, during the day. I don't care if you have to reschedule your workday. I don't care if you have to leave earlier or come home later. I don't care if you have to have one less business appointment during the day. What matters is your taking the trouble to go outside and move in the light. Your health, your sanity, and your entire future are at stake.

"There are other things I want you to do just because they also create stress for you. I want to see you change your diet to eliminate sweets and other junk foods. I want you to stop smoking and cut down on your drinking. It won't be painful. The same plan I give my patients who have tranquilizer addiction will work for you. The choline and other vitamins will work just as well for someone whose habit is smoking as it will for someone craving a Valium.

"Now I want you to do this for a month, that's all. At the end of that time, if you still feel the same way about things, then leave New York, your wife, and your family. Start life over again with some girl in Big Sur. Do whatever is your dream, no matter how much anyone might disagree, since that will be what is right for you. But first I want you to give my suggestion a chance. What do you say?"

"I think that's fair. A month I can handle, though I have a feeling it won't change anything."

George had a right to be skeptical. He had designed a lifestyle to give him an important public image. He admitted to me later that he always wanted to be viewed as a sensitive and intelligent individual, hard-working but cerebral rather than physical. He wanted to be known as a dedicated thinker, which was why he spent so much time at the office. A certain amount of outdoor activity is essential for human emotional survival. George discovered this himself.

"I can't believe the change your plan made. I took a long walk on the way back to the office the very first day. It was right after I had seen you and I felt marvelous. I was relaxed and happy, though I blamed the feeling on my decision to try your plan before leaving. However, the next day, after my walk, I felt just as good. And that feeling continued.

"I didn't try the rest of your plan until that weekend because I really thought it was all a lot of nonsense. In fact, if you hadn't told me to very gradually reduce my smoking, I wouldn't have tried that part at all. But you know, all my desires to run away have disappeared. I take time off during the day but it seems to make me more efficient on the job. I'm doing more in less time, so I actually accomplish more than ever while spending fewer hours in the office.

"Something else happened too. My wife says I now have the passion of a teenager. I never realized how biochemically upset I was from lack of sunlight. My life was just plain unhealthy. I am a new man now. I'm outdoors during the daylight and my life is balanced between the mental and the physical."

You have seen how many have learned to change their lives and have found the path to freedom from chemical dependency.

You will never endure greater physical and mental confusion than during this time of weaning from chemical dependence. After you have passed through the withdrawal stage, you should continue to start each day with a multiple vitamin/mineral tablet without copper.

Most people need at least 2500 mg of Vitamin C, spread throughout the day. This should be a regular supplement. The minimum supplement must be 1500 mg. Additional C, 1000 mg at a time, can be added under special stress. During periods of extreme stress, illness, personal tragedy, and life crises, increase your dose to 5000 to 7000 mg (5 to 7 grams).

My clients tell me that they keep three different vitamin bottles in their desk. One is a container of Vitamin C. The second is niacinamide and the third is choline. The choline is taken when they feel so overwhelmed that they crave an escape through smoking or tranquilizers. The niacinamide is usually either the 500-mg or 1000-mg size, and they take as many as necessary. If the situation they encounter seems overwhelming, they take 2000 to 3000 mg.

A minimum dose of panthothenic acid should be 1000 mg. In extra-stressful situations, take an additional 500 to 1000 mg.

Vitamin B complex should be taken in the 100 mg quantity discussed earlier. Again this is a stress vitamin. The normal dose, a single pill, contains 100 mg of each of the B complex vitamins. This can be doubled or tripled as your situation warrants.

My former patients have learned to experiment with the vitamins during periods of stress. They follow the basic supplements but increase the dose as they feel extraordinary anxiety. They have learned that when the pressures of the day seem overwhelming, it is likely that they are nutritionally deficient in niacinamide, pantothenic acid, choline, Vitamin C, and the B's.

Zinc comes conveniently in 50-mg tablets, two of which should be taken each day. You will find from 50 to 100 mg an average dose and should take more only when you are having skin problems or sex problems, or to promote wound healing. Men should consume 800 IU of Vitamin E daily, women 600. Areas such as Los Angeles, Washington, D.C., Baltimore, New York, and similarly polluted cities require an increase in zinc and Vitamin E to help the body deal with poisons from pollution.

Lecithin granules should continue to be a part of your daily diet, because each tablespoon contains 500 mg of choline. A 1000-mg tablet of pantothenic acid should also be routine. You should also keep your dolomite or L-tryptophane handy for when you are having difficulty sleeping.

Continue exercising and meditating every day, and increase the exercise when you are under high stress and need to work out your problems. Visualization exercises are excellent reinforcers of positive goals and should be used at least once a week during meditation.

Talking-it-out can be a routine part of your day, a way of ventilating anxieties as they come up. If you have an ongoing, open relationship with another person, sharing your concerns each day can maintain and strengthen your closeness. You will find when you're off tranquilizers you are strong enough to make positive changes.

Not all coupled relationships endure. Sometimes one partner outgrows the other. When your life takes such a turn, separation is actually a positive step.

If you feel at odds with your colleagues or your employer, changing jobs might be the answer for you. If your apartment is surrounded by neighbors whose loud music and inconsiderate parties are keeping you from sleeping, or if your space is so cramped, cluttered, and poorly lighted that you feel emotionally and physically restricted, again a change may be in order.

Leaving the familiar is always difficult, even when the familiar is making you miserable. By taking a positive step for change, you give yourself a chance to grow. Others may disagree with your decision but they are not living your life. Change is a way of handling stress that you cannot or may not wish to adapt to.

Remember that you are unique. You have worth. You have value. You are the most important person you know and you must be comfortable with yourself before you can be comfortable with others. Your life cannot be judged by the lives of those around you.

There is no way to avoid the problems of life. Even the most perfect existence is going to be interrupted by the loss of loved ones, the breakdown of mechanical objects just when we need them most, and all the other traumas and minor irritants everyone must face. But our lives are enriched if we work positively with stress. By using vitamins, meditation, talking-it-out, and exercise and giving yourself maximum nutrition, you will find yourself happier, healthier, able to contribute more to the world than you ever imagined was possible. Armed with the plan I have set forth—a plan that has already helped so many—and with the follow-up method for coping with stress, you will truly be able to say—once and for all—"Goodbye, Blues."

Appendix 1

Where to Turn for Additional Information and Help

Readers who would like more information on the topics discussed in this book or would like guidance through the program, might wish to contact the organizations listed below. They have information, and names of people around the country whose approach will likely be similar to mine.

The Huxley Institute for Bio-Social Research, 1114 First Avenue, New York, New York 10022. Telephone 212-759-9554.

Pills Anonymous, 443 West 50th Street, New York, New York 10019. An organization with branches throughout the United States.

National Clearing House for Drug Abuse, P.O. Box 1706, Rockville, Maryland 20852.

National Clearing House for Alcohol Information, P.O. Box 2345, Rockville, Maryland 20852.

Director of Communications, Office of Alcoholism and Substance Abuse, New York State Division of Substance Abuse Services, Executive Park, Box 8200, Albany, New York 12203.

Fryer Research Center, 200 West 57th Street, New York, New York 10019. Telephone 212-265-5805.

Appendix 2
Some Dietary Guidelines

The foods you eat are potent factors in relieving or creating stress for your body. By structuring your diet according to the following recommendations during the period you are withdrawing from tranquilizers or other nonessential prescription drugs, you will find that you will have a much easier time. After the withdrawal period, you can feel free to cheat *provided you basically maintain a good diet.* Some information relating to which vitamins to take when you do cheat are included at the end of this appendix.

Meat, Fish, Fowl: Meats in general, and especially organ meats, are good for you. Fish and poultry are healthier than beef, but meat should be a part of your regular diet. Liver, organ meats, oysters, salmon, and eggs are all rich in Vitamin B_{12} and might be classed as energy foods.

Vegetables: Among the best vegetables for my plan are asparagus, avocado, beets, broccoli, Brussel sprouts, cabbage, carrots, cauliflower, celery, cucumber, eggplant, green beans, lettuce, lima beans, onions, radishes, sauerkraut, squash, string beans, tomatoes, turnips, and zucchini.

166

Fruits: Among the best fruits are apricots, berries, grapefruit, melons, oranges, peaches, pears, pineapples, and tangerines. These should be eaten raw or may be cooked. They must be taken without cream or sugar. If the fruit is purchased canned, make certain it is in a water pack with no sugar added. Fruit in syrup is always sugared.

Juices: Any unsweetened fruit or vegetable juice is generally good for you. The exceptions are grape juice and prune juice, both of which have a high sugar content.

Beverages: Weak tea, herbal tea, coffee substitutes (Pero, Postum, etc.); Sanka, Brim, and other decaffeinated coffee.

Desserts: Fresh fruits, nuts, seeds, soybeans, cheese. Avoid pies, cake, candy, and other sugar products.

Steer Clear of: Biscuits, cakes, cookies, pies, white rice, French fries, corn (high natural sugar content), spaghetti, while bread and white-flour recipes, noodles, macaroni, cookies, honey, hard liquor, red wines, soft drinks, beer, bananas, starchy beans, cordials, cocktails. White wine is generally the wine with the lowest sugar content, but even this should be avoided while you are withdrawing from tranquilizers.

A baked potato with full skin is good for you. So is brown rice. If you have never eaten brown rice, it looks very much like processed rice and is not actually brown in color. It is slightly darker when compared side by side with processed rice. What is important is that it is a nutritious, whole food that has not been robbed of vitamins.

If you want a special diet, you can use your imagination when selecting from the foods included in the above list as well as those foods high in the various vitamins. Remember that cooking can destroy some of the nutrition. Don't overcook, and whenever possible eat your fruits and vegetables raw.

Some of my patients like to use the following menu as a guide. They substitute freely, but use this as a way of ensuring that they fulfill all of their bodies' basic nutritional needs daily:

Breakfast: Fruit, one or two eggs, cheese, or fish, one slice of whole-rye or whole-wheat bread or toast (read ingredients on package; look for bread without sugar or preservatives), and a beverage. You can have a small amount of butter, but remember that jelly is a sugar product.

Two hours after breakfast: 4 ounces of grapefruit juice.

Lunch: Meat, cheese, or fish. Salad with a large serving of lettuce and tomato, plus other raw vegetables from the list. Salad dressing can be safflower oil and vinegar or lemon juice. Vegetables from the list, one slice of rye bread or toast and butter. You can have a dessert as listed and a beverage.

Three hours after lunch: Protein snack. You can have eggs, sardines, nuts, or other protein foods of your choosing.

One hour before dinner: 4 ounces of grapefruit juice.

Dinner: Soup if desired. Make certain it is not thickened with flour and contains no sugar. Vegetables; a portion of meat, fish, or poultry; one slice of whole-wheat or whole-rye bread as desired. Dessert selected from the list and a beverage.

Three hours after dinner: Protein snack of your choosing.

If desired, take a small quantity of nuts every two hours from dinner until bedtime.

Some foods contain natural calmatives such as L-tryptophane and the B vitamins. Among these are whole milk, soy milk, fish, beef, soy flour, organ meats, shellfish, and eggs. Magnesium is found in soy flour, whole wheat, oatmeal, peas, brown rice, whole corn, beans, and nuts.

Early in the book I mentioned a pep-up drink some of my patients enjoy taking each morning. This is a beverage containing 1 teaspoon of brewer's yeast powder or brewer's yeast flakes, 1 teaspoon of protein powder, 1 teaspoon of dry skim milk powder, and 1 teaspoon of lecithin granules. Shake this in a shaker or mix in a blender with milk or tomato juice. Remember, however, that some people find this beverage unpalatable. They prefer to simply eat lecithin granules either from the jar or sprinkled on salads. The granules have an agreeable nutty flavor.

I mentioned cheating on the diet once you are past the withdrawal stage. I am not a fanatic when it comes to eating. I know full well that you are going to want to take an occasional alcoholic beverage, eat a piece of pie or cake, and otherwise depart from this diet. My attitude is that you should go ahead and indulge yourself occasionally—but recognize that you are adding stress to your body. Treat the resulting stress in the following way:

Whenever you deviate from my plan by having pie, cake, cookies, a drink, or whatever, take 500 mg of pantothenic acid and 1000 mg of Vitamin C. You should take the same when you have a cup of normal coffee, adding 1000 mg of niacinamide as well. Since coffee is a stimulant, the extra niacinamide acts to calm you.

On Digesting Vitamin and Mineral Pills: Some people have difficulty swallowing pills. I suggest that you put the pills in a blender and add milk with some flavorings such as ice cream with honey, a drop of vanilla, and cinnamon to disguise the taste.

If you experience nausea after taking vitamins, try eating fresh fruit, particularly papaya or pineapple, which act as digestive aids. Any food or thick beverage taken with the vitamins helps break them down.

Bibliography

Adams, Ruth and Murray, Frank, Megavitamin Therapy. New York. Larchmont Books, 1973.

Assagioli, Roberto, Act of Will. New York: Viking, 1973.

Assagioli, Roberto, Psychosynthesis New York: Hobbs-Dorman, 1965.

Benson, Herbert, The Relaxation Response. New York: William Morrow, 1976.

Brown, Barbara, New Mind, New Body. New York: Harper & Row, 1976.

Cheraskin, E., W. Ringspore, and J. W. Clarke, Diet and Disease. New Canaan: Keats Publishing, 1968.

Davis, Adelle, Let's Get Well. New York: Harcourt Brace Jovanovich, 1965.

Dubos, Rene, Mirage of Health. New York: Harper & Row, 1959.

Frank, Jerome, Persuasion and Healing. Baltimore: Johns Hopkins University Press, 1961.

Fredericks, Carleton and Henry Goodman, Low Blood Sugar and You. New York: Constellation Internal, 1969.

Gordon, Barbara, I'm Dancing As Fast As I Can. New York: Harper & Row, 1979.

Hawkins, Harold, Applied Nutrition. Los Angeles: Ca. International College of Applied Nutrition, 1947.

Hoffer, Abram, *Orthomolecular Nutrition*. New Canaan: Keats Publishing, 1978.

Hughes, Richard and Robert Brewin, *The Tranquilizing of America*. New York: Harcourt Brace Jovanovich, 1979.

Huxley, Aldous, *The Doors of Perception*. London: Chatto & Windus, 1959.

Illich, Ivan, *Medical Nemesis*. New York: Pantheon, 1976.

Jung, Carl G., *Archetypes and Collective Unconscious*. Princeton: Princeton University Press, 1964.

Koestler, Arthur, *The Ghost in the Machine*. New York: Macmillan, 1967.

Kostrubala, Thaddeus, *The Joy of Running*. New York: Lippincott, 1970.

Lappé, Frances Moore, *Diet for a Small Planet*. New York: Ballantine, 1971.

Lilliston, Lynn, *Megavitamins: A New Key to Health*. New York: Fawcett, 1975.

Lilly, John, *The Center of the Cyclone*. New York: Julian Press, 1972.

Pauwels, Louis and Jacques Bergier, *Morning of the Magicians*. Paris: Editions Gallimard, 1960.

Pfeiffer, Carl, *Mental and Elemental Nutrients, A Physicians' Guide to Nutrition and Health Care*. New Canaan: Keats Publishing, 1975.

Poole, Mary Jane, ed., *House and Garden Book of Total Health*. New York: G. P. Putnam, 1978.

Prevention Staff, *Complete Book of Vitamins*. Emmaus: Rodale Books, 1977.

Reich, Wilhelm, *Character Analysis*. New York: Orgone Press, 1949.

Rodale, J., *Health Seeker*. Emmaus: Rodale Books, 1967.

Rubincam, David, *Diet with Vitamins*. New York: A & W Publishers, 1977.

Selye, Hans, *Stress without Distress*. New York: Lippincott, 1974.

Skinner, B. F., *Walden Two*. New York: Macmillan, 1974.

Szasz, Thomas, *The Myth of Mental Illness*. New York: Harper & Row, 1974.

Toffler, Alvin, *Future Shock*. New York: Random House, 1970.

Torrey, E. Fuller, *The Death of Psychiatry*. Radnor: Chilton Book Co., 1974.

Wade, Carlson, *Magic Minerals*. New York: Parker Publishing, 1971.

Watson, George, *Nutrition and Your Mind*. New York: Harper & Row, 1972.

Webb, Wilse B, Sleep: The Gentle Tyrant. New York: Prentice-Hall, 1975.

Whitmont, Edward, The Symbolic Quest. New York: Putnam, for the C. G. Jung Foundation for Analytic Psychology, 1970.

Whyte, L. I., The Next Development in Man. New York: Holt, 1948.

Yudkin, John, Sweet and Dangerous. New York: Wyden Publishing, 1972.